HOW THE BLOOD WORKS

Vision Publishing, P.O. Box 11166, Carson, Calif. 90746-1166

The Lord gave the word: great was the company of those that published it.
— **Psalm 68:11**

Vision Publishing
P.O. Box 11166
Carson, CA 90746-1166

Design and Typography by Words & Pictures Press, Tustin, CA

**Publisher's Cataloging in Publication
(Prepared by Quality Books Inc.)**

Williford, Stanley O.
    How the blood works : understanding the laws that govern the blood / Stanley O. Williford.
    p. cm.

    1. Jesus Christ—Blood—Biblical teaching. I. Title.
BT590.B5W55 1996   232
                        QB196-20477

DEDICATION

*I dedicate this book to
my Lord Jesus Christ,
to my wife, Corliss,
and to our children,
Steve, Nicole, Brian and Brandon*

ACKNOWLEDGEMENTS

What a blessing it has been to sit
at the feet of a wonderful pastor,
teacher and man of God,
Dr. Frederick K.C. Price,
for the past 16 years.
Any good that is seen in this work
is a reflection of his teaching.

CONTENTS

THANKS

A special note of thanks to
all the encouraging voices who believed in what
I was doing and urged me on.
I particularly would like to thank Pat Hays
for her incisive editorial suggestions,
Jerold Potter, himself a publisher, of Word of Faith and
Power Ministry, for publishing ideas, and
Minister Argie Taylor for her prayers.
Keni Davis of Keni Arts was a
constant voice of friendship.
Among the mighty cloud of witnesses in glory,
the voice of my mother, Mary E. Williford,
is one of constant support.
Thanks, Momma, for the cheers.

INTRODUCTION

Blood is a fluid tissue that circulates through our bodies, feeding the cells, and hauling away the carbonic refuse that the cells throw off. It is the system of transport for the body. The blood is propelled at the rate of about three feet per second by the powerful force of the heart. It makes the complete circuit of the body in about 30 second's time, and in the process covers upward of 60,000 miles of blood vessels. Not one cell escapes contact with the blood.

The blood is the life-carrier that nourishes and enlivens the body, which is the instrument of life. While the blood needs the body to keep it contained, the body would be an empty, lifeless, rotting shell without this precious fluid coursing through it.

I believe the study of human blood is as important to the Church as it is to medicine or science because the work it does in our human bodies parallels the work the blood of Jesus does in the Body of Christ. Also, it is the medium of exchange between the physical and spirit worlds. This knowledge came to me by revelation, but it was evidently common knowledge to primitive man, as such books as *The Blood Covenant* by H. Clay Trumbull attest.

To this day, many societies practice forms of blood covenanting between friends and between those who seek alliances or protection from one another. Why? Because they believe that there is no closer bond that can be established between men than becoming blood brothers through the mixing, tasting, drinking or the exchange of one another's blood. It has something to do with the mysterious life-sharing properties of the blood.

The recent publication of such books as "The Blood" by Benny Hinn, "The Word, the Name, the Blood" by Joyce Meyer, and "The Blood and the Glory" by Billye Brim, and others, suggest that the Church is putting more emphasis on understanding the all-important subject of the Blood of Jesus. I believe that in combining these two disciplines — the study of the natural and the supernatural works of blood — we can develop a more perfect understanding of what our blood and His blood accomplishes.

Part of the reason why this book has been written is to create dialogue, to stir more thinking along spiritual bloodlines. I have written what I believe the Lord has given me on blood, and I have merged that with the Word of God, and with other information gained from reading on the subject. I make no pretense at being an expert on blood either spiritually or scientifically, but I do believe that what is written between these covers is very significant and will aid some in understanding our "fearfully and wonderfully made" bodies, as well as human blood and the Blood of Jesus.

Before you read further, let's establish two premises: First, that "the life of the flesh is in the blood" (Lev. 17:11) and, second, that all life flows from God. Blood is what transports that life.

Stanley O. Williford
1996

HOW THE BLOOD WORKS

Understanding the laws that govern the Blood

By Stanley O. Williford,
as revealed by The Holy Spirit

ONE

NO SIN, NO BLOOD

Sin introduced us to blood. Through the knowledge of sin came the knowledge of blood. Blood became significant to man only after the entrance of sin into the world. Had Adam not sinned, the world would never have heard of blood, the blood sacrifice, or a blood covenant. All blood would have remained perfectly encased in the envelope of the body, and we would never have seen its too-familiar stain.

In fact, you cannot have sin without blood. Where

sin is, blood must be present as well. Blood must be shed where sin is if life is to be maintained. Blood will either be shed to cover sin, or it will be shed wantonly — and increasingly — in sin.

In the natural world, when blood appears it is usually as a physical reaction to a wound or some other harm to the body. Blood covers the wound and immediately starts the healing process. Every element in blood springs into action at the first sign of a rupture or attack. Every alarm in it is sounded and survival of the body becomes the main concern. Blood's protective instincts marshal the infection fighters, and clotting agents begin to mass around the wound or infection. The cleansing, healing and sealing of the wound begins to take place.

In the spirit world, sin is the wound and blood is a spiritual reaction to it. When there is sin, it will always result in bloodshed (death) whether the bloodshed was intentional or not. This is the wage that sin pays. In fact, the more sin is prevalent, the more blood will be shed. This fact is irrefutable; it cannot be changed. So then we can establish a law — **The Law of Sin and Blood**, which says: *Where there is sin, there must be blood* — and its reciprocal, which says, *If there is no sin, there will be no blood.* Put another way, the law says: *If there is sin, blood must be shed to pay for it. For the wages of sin is death* (Rom. 6:23).

Down through human history, from Adam to Moses, when man sinned, blood flowed. It was either the blood of animals, where man sought atonement (a covering from the judgment that was to come), or the blood of man. All shed blood, whether man or animal, is the result of sin.

When Moses brought the Law, a type of order was established. Man, with his fallen nature, could not be held accountable for sin where there was no law. God had to institute a law, a standard by which man could live. These verses in Romans tell us that:

Romans 5:12-14:

> **Wherefore, as by one man sin entered into the world, and death by sin; and so death passed upon all men, for that all have sinned:**

> **(For until the law sin was in the world: but sin is not imputed** [counted against you] **when there is no law.**

> **Nevertheless death reigned from Adam to Moses, even over them that had not sinned after the similitude of Adam's transgression, who is the figure of him that was to come.**

Because of Adam's sin, death reigned — and blood flowed — until the Law was instituted. After the Law, death was no longer in control — as long as men kept the Law. Part of the Law was the offering of blood.

Blood Indicates Something Is Wrong

When we see blood we know that something is wrong. There is a problem in the body. Alarms go off in the physical body when it is wounded, and alarms go off in the spirit when sin is committed. The offering of the blood sacrifice was man's recognition that something was wrong spiritually and his effort to make atonement for it.

We can easily draw the inference from Genesis 3:21 that when Adam sinned, God drew first blood. It was a spiritual response indicating that something was wrong.

That blood carried a type of spiritual cleansing, healing and sealing, but the shedding of it had to be done physically. By right, one would think, it should have been Adam and Eve's blood that was shed rather than some innocent animal's. And one would be quite right to think that.

But though it was Adam and Eve who had sinned, their blood could not have been used. Adam and Eve's blood, being no longer innocent, had become spiritually ineffective. In fact, all human blood became tainted because of their transgression, which is the active breaking of God's law. Adam and Eve's blood was tainted because of sin. Had either one of them not sinned, man might have somehow had a chance to hold on to his innocent nature. I believed that God would have honored the innocent one and saved the guilty.

In fact, it is a principle used extensively in the Bible that when a believer and unbeliever are somehow joined together, the unbeliever can be saved or sanctified by the believer, as the following Scripture states:

1st Cor. 7:14:

For the unbelieving husband is sanctified by the wife, and the unbelieving wife is sanctified by the husband: else were your children unclean; but now are they holy.

Since Adam and Eve both had sinned, it is a moot point, but consider the alternative: If Adam had lived up to the standard of life he had been taught by his Father, he would have sanctified Eve and mankind would have been saved. But with both having sinned, their coming together sexually produced "unclean" children and perpetuated the sinful nature. These actions clearly doomed mankind.

14

God had to provide innocent blood to close the spiritual breach and start the healing process. He literally had to forestall man's destruction by intervening with lifesaving blood. So He turned to the animal kingdom and began the first animal sacrifice. Now we can see the law's relationship to the first sin, which resulted in the first blood.

Gen. 3:21:

Unto Adam also and to his wife did the Lord God make coats of skins, and clothed them.

"Coats (tunics) of skins" mean that some animal died to provide the covering for Adam and Eve's nakedness. (Nakedness here is simply a metaphor for sin.) Prior to sin, they had no such requirement for apparel. The pair were "clothed" in a spirit covering, for it is clear that before they sinned their nakedness never mattered to them. They were hardly aware of it. The Bible tells us in Gen. 2:25 that they were naked and were not ashamed.

After sin, Adam and Eve became conscious of their nakedness and ran to make clothing of fig leaves. Rather than being God-conscious, they sank to self-consciousness, which is tantamount to sin-consciousness. God was replaced as the center of their focus and the ever-expanding, ever-lusting self ascended to the throne of their lives. They began to view their nakedness as something to hide in shame.

The Type Of Sin Doesn't Matter

We do not know exactly what fruit Adam and Eve ate, or what sin it represented. Could it have been literal fruit, representing only simple disobedience? Could it

15

have represented some sexual sin? Should we even be concerned? No, we should not. Because, ultimately, it doesn't matter what sin it was. Any sin, no matter what it was, would have had the same effect. Adam was on such a high level with God that he had no excuse for ever missing the mark. Adam was a god-man.

Here's what's important: It was the first sin, and from it sprang all other sins. All Satan needed was a first sin to ignite the fire that would kindle all latter sins. He found that spark in Adam and Eve. So we can see clearly that Adam and Eve (at Satan's insistence) gave birth to human sin. They also gave birth to the first natural humans, who were born under the sign of sin.

It is difficult for us today to contemplate a world without sin because we have never known such a dimension. Adam lived in a pure world, outside of time. Since Adam, this type of world has been beyond human experience. It is obvious that if Adam had not sinned, our present world would be a very different place. It would be like Eden. It would be like heaven. There would be no Satan to contend with, and no demons. There would be no sickness and no disease. There would be no poverty and lack. There would be no suffering, prejudice, ignorance, lying, hate, or death. There would be no bloodshed, and Jesus would still be walking and talking with man in the cool of the day.

But Adam did sin, and that sin tore a breach in the spirit world that left man on one side and God on the other. Through that breach came a host of ungodly elements to infect man's spirit, his conscience, his body, his family, his home, and his environment. That first sin opened a divide so wide in God's creation that Adam and all the blood shed until Jesus could never close it.

Only God's blood could close it.

This condition was Adam's legacy to his children.

Let's return to the first blood.

Gen. 3:21:

Unto Adam also and to his wife did the Lord God make coats of skins, and clothed them.

The concept of a covering for Adam and Eve's bodies was less immediate to God than the covering for their sin. It was the blood of those animals that had to be released, not their coats of skin. Several writers have suggested that Adam and Eve wore these skins while they were still wet with blood because they needed a spiritual covering, not a physical covering. (It is reminiscent of Jesus on the cross, where he became sin for us. Jesus became our sin and then covered that sin with His own innocent blood.)

When God went to the animal kingdom to draw blood — for without blood, there would have been no covering of Adam's sin — Satan was temporarily thwarted. Sin left uncovered, spreads like contagion. The act of covering, brings control, containment, conviction. (Every born-again person has a covering, which is the blood of Jesus. Those without Him have no covering, no protection from the effects of sin but what they can devise.)

Satan's mission was to create havoc and destroy control and order, to bring death to God's highest creation. He wanted Adam's death, so he wanted Adam to sin. After Adam sinned, Satan wanted that sin uncovered. The longer sin remained uncovered, the more havoc it would cause and the sooner Adam's time would be up.

When God showed Adam how to use blood to cover sin, Satan struck back by getting Cain, Adam's son, to defy the offering of blood to cover sin.

Let's quickly review the story: Cain and Abel were brothers, sons of Adam. Cain was a tiller of the ground, Abel a shepherd. Abel brought a "firstling" from his flock, "and of the fat thereof," but Cain brought grains, fruit or vegetables — something ridiculous that God could not accept. Even logic told Cain he was wrong. God did not need food; He is God. Any offering we bring to God is for our own benefit. God wanted Cain to have the experience of taking life to cover sin, to have the realization of the cause-and-effect relationship between sin and death. The blood wasn't for God's pleasure. God is not bloodthirsty. Blood was the only thing He could accept as a covering for sin, and Cain knew that.

Gen. 4:4-5:

> **. . . And the Lord had respect unto Abel and to his offering:**
>
> **But unto Cain and to his offering he had not respect. And Cain was very wroth, and his countenance fell.**

One of the meanings of *wroth* is to "blaze up" in anger. Cain was so angry that his anger blazed. His countenance turned virtually upside down.

Now look at those two verses again. Genesis 4:4 tells us that the "Lord had *respect* unto Abel and to his offering," but Verse 5 says He had *no respect* unto Cain and to his offering. Cain had not respected the Lord in the type of offering he brought, so the Lord could not return respect to him. That is what made Cain angry, not his brother, Abel. Cain was angry at God, and his anger was unwarranted. Cain knew God required a blood sacrifice, and yet he refused to offer it.

God warns Cain and attempts to mollify his anger with reason and love. God asks, in Verses 6-7:

> **. . . Why art thou wroth? and why is thy countenance fallen?**

> **If thou doest well, shalt thou not be accepted? and if thou doest not well, sin lieth at the door. And unto thee shall be his desire, and thou shalt rule over him.**

Friend, I love those verses. They demonstrate to me the character and gentleness of our loving Father. He had every reason to be angry with Cain, but there He was trying to soothe Cain's anger, to tenderly teach him. And yet there is more than a hint of firmness in His words. It was obvious that Cain had not done "well," but the Lord tells him that *if* he does do well and brings the proper sacrifice, it will be accepted, just as Abel's was.

Here is my interpretation: *"In other words, Cain, you must bring what is required, and bring it in the right attitude. I have no preference for Abel over you, but you must come in faith, as Abel did. If you refuse, your anger will allow sin to come in and get control over you, but you should be controlling it. As for your anger, I am the Lord God, and I will not change."*

Now we can see how unbridled anger can turn to sin. Anger is a breeding ground for sin, especially unrighteous, prideful anger. Remember, the law says where there is sin blood will follow.

Gen. 4:8:

> **And Cain talked** [quarreled] **with Abel his brother: and it came to pass, when they**

were in the field, that Cain rose up against Abel his brother, and slew him.

Thus, the first human blood was shed, and the equation that says sin equals blood comes into play again. Sin cannot help but end in bloodshed, either animal or man. Uncovered and unconfessed sin will eventually result in man's bloodshed, as happened with Cain and Abel. If Cain had offered blood, Abel would have remained alive. There is no covering for sin other than blood.

Lev. 17:11:

For the life of the flesh is in the blood: and I have given it to you upon the altar to make an atonement for your souls: for it is the blood [death of the sacrifice] **that maketh an atonement for the soul.**

By the time of the events of Genesis 6, sin had become so great and violence so widespread on the earth that virtually all men and animals had to perish in the flood. The Cains of the world, those who refused to acknowledge God by the offering of blood, had allowed sin to get out of control. As has already been stated, blood brings control, containment, conviction. Where none is offered, sin flourishes. If Cain had been obedient and offered the sacrifice of blood, sin would have been contained, at least temporarily. Obedience would have made his heart tender, and he would not have slain his brother. Instead, he goes off to Nod and begins to replenish the earth with his kind.

Gen. 6: 5,7:

And God saw that the wickedness of man was great in the earth, and that every imagi-

nation of the thoughts of his heart was only evil continually. . . .

And the Lord said, I will destroy man whom I have created from the face of the earth; both man, and beast, and the creeping thing, and the fowls of the air; for it repenteth me that I have made them.

When the ark landed and Noah and his family disembarked, the first thing Noah did was to offer a blood sacrifice to God to purify the earth again.

Gen. 8:20:

And Noah builded an altar unto the Lord; and took of every clean beast, and of every clean fowl, and offered burnt offerings on the altar.

Sin had to be covered to stop its spread, but the men of Noah's time refused to cover it. The Bible tells us in Hebrews that "without the shedding of blood is no remission" of sin (Heb. 9:22). This is a spiritual law from which the Law of Sin and Blood flows. God took the occasion of the first transgression to teach Adam that blood was necessary to remit his sin. That knowledge was passed down through his generations, but from Cain down men began to disregard it.

H.A. Maxwell Whyte, in his excellent book, *The Power of the Blood,* records that after sin no other clothing but that procured by the death of animals would have sufficed for Adam. He writes:

"So animals were slaughtered, and after the blood was shed, Adam and Eve were covered with the skins. The principle of a life

21

for a life runs throughout the Bible. No
other garments would sufficiently cover
Adam and Eve except those which involved
the shedding of blood." [1]

We also know that God is not a waster. He shed the
blood, used the animal skins for Adam and Eve's clothing, and even allowed man to eat of the flesh. Man eventually became a meat-eater, probably for the first time
after eating of a sacrifice. It is clear, however, that each
of these activities fall far below the divine standard that
God had set for man in Eden. Blood for sin, skin for
clothing and flesh for food were not part of the original
plan. God's best was no sin, spirit for covering, and herbs
(Gen. 1:29) and communion with Almighty God for food.
But a new, lower standard became necessary after man
fell from his godlike heights.

Unification With God

The eating of the sacrifice became a way to show
unification and communion with God. It was as if God
himself had been slain and man was allowed to partake
of His nature by eating the flesh. We see this in Exodus
12 where the Lord tells Israel to take a lamb "without
blemish, a male of the first year" and kill it. Then Israel
was instructed to "take of the blood, and strike it on the
two side posts and on the upper door posts of the houses,
wherein they shall *eat it.*"

"The flesh of the chosen lamb was to be eaten by the
Israelites, reverently, as an indication of that inter-communion [with God]," [2] writes H. Clay Trumbull in *The
Blood Covenant,* his monumental work that was written
more than 100 years ago.

The practice became prevalent in primitive societies

"everywhere," notes Trumbull: "Because those animals became, as it were, on the altar, or on the table, of the gods, a portion of the gods themselves, they must not be eaten except by those who discerned in them the body of the gods, and who were entitled to share them in inter-communion with the gods." [3]

After the price of sin was paid at the cross, all blood but the blood of Jesus lost its spiritual significance as the agent for covering sin. Jesus' blood accomplished remission of sin for all time. It became both the ultimate covering and the ultimate healer. It established a New Covenant between man and God, a covenant better than the one that biblical Israel resided under. That covenant is written in Jesus' blood. To see this clearly, I believe we need to read Hebrews, Chapter 9, in its entirety. Here, I am quoting from the Amplified Bible. There is great revelatory power in these verses.

> **Now even the first covenant had its own rules *and* regulations for divine worship, and it had a sanctuary, [but one] of this world.** [Exod. 25:10-40.]
>
> **For a tabernacle (tent) was erected, in the outer division *or* compartment of which were the lampstand and the table with [its loaves of] the showbread set forth. [This portion] is called the Holy [Place].** [Lev. 24:5,6.]
>
> **But [inside], beyond the second curtain *or* veil, [there stood another] tabernacle [division] known as the Holy of Holies.** [Exod. 26:31-33.]
>
> **It had the golden altar of incense and the**

ark (chest) of the covenant, covered over with wrought gold. This [ark] contained a golden jar which held the manna, and the rod of Aaron that sprouted, and the [two stone] slabs of the covenant, [bearing the Ten Commandments]. [Exod. 30:1-6; 16:32-34; Num. 17:8-10.]

Above [the ark] and overshadowing the mercy seat were the representations of the cherubim [winged creatures which were the symbols] of glory. We cannot now go into detail about these things.

These arrangements having thus been made, the priests enter habitually into the outer division of the tabernacle, in performance of their ritual acts of worship.

But into the second [division of the tabernacle] none but the high priest goes, and he only once a year, and never without taking a sacrifice of blood with him, which he offers for himself and for the errors *and* sins of ignorance *and* thoughtlessness which the people have committed. [Lev. 16:15.]

By this the Holy Spirit points out that the way into the [true Holy of] Holies is not yet thrown open as long as the former [the outer portion of the] tabernacle remains a recognized institution *and* is still standing,

Seeing that that first [outer portion of the] tabernacle was a parable — a visible symbol or type or picture of the present age. In it gifts and sacrifices are offered, and yet are incapable of perfecting the conscience *or* of cleansing *and* renewing the inner man of the worshipper.

For [the ceremonies] deal only with clean and unclean meats and drinks and different washings, [mere] external rules *and* regulations for the body imposed to tide the worshippers over until the time of setting things straight — of reformation, [of the complete new order when Christ, the Messiah, shall establish the reality of what these things foreshadow, a better covenant].

But [that appointed time came] when Christ, the Messiah, appeared as a High Priest of the better things that have come *and* are to come. [Then] through the greater and more perfect tabernacle, not made with [human] hands, that is, not a part of this material creation,

He went once for all into the [Holy of] Holies [of heaven], not by virtue of the blood of goats and calves [by which to make reconciliation between God and man], but His own blood, having found *and* secured a complete redemption — an everlasting release [for us].

For if [the mere] sprinkling of unholy *and* defiled persons with blood of goats and bulls and with the ashes of a burnt heifer is sufficient for the purification of the body, [Lev. 16:6,16; Num. 19:9, 17, 18.]

How much more surely shall the blood of Christ, Who by virtue of [His] eternal Spirit [His own pre-existent divine personality] has offered Himself an unblemished sacrifice to God, purify our consciences from dead works *and* lifeless observances to serve the [ever-] living God?

[Christ, the Messiah] is therefore the Negotiator *and* Mediator of an [entirely] new agreement (testament, covenant), so that those who are called *and* offered it, may receive the fulfillment of the promised everlasting inheritance, since a death has taken place which rescues *and* delivers *and* redeems them from the transgressions committed under the [old], first agreement.

For where there is a [last] will *and* testament involved, the death of the one who made it must be established,

For a will *and* testament is valid and takes effect only at death, since it has no force *or* legal power as long as the one who made it is alive.

So even the (old) first covenant [God's will] was not inaugurated *and* ratified *and* put in force without the shedding of blood.

For when every command of the Law had been read out by Moses to all the people, he took the blood of slain calves and goats, together with water and scarlet wool, and with a bunch of hyssop sprinkled both the Book [the roll of the Law and covenant] itself, and all the people,

Saying these words: This is the blood that seals *and* ratifies the agreement (the testament, the covenant) which God commanded [me to deliver to] you. [Exod. 24:6-8.]

And in the same way he sprinkled with the blood both the tabernacle and all the [sacred] vessels *and* appliances used in [divine] worship.

[In fact], under the Law almost everything is purified by means of blood, and without the shedding of blood there is neither release from sin and its guilt *nor* the remission of the due *and* merited punishment for sins.

By such means therefore it was necessary for the [earthly] copies of the heavenly things to be purified, but the actual heavenly things themselves [required far] better *and* nobler sacrifices than these.

For Christ, the Messiah, has not entered into a sanctuary made with [human] hands, only a copy *and* pattern *and* type of the true one, but [He has entered] into heaven itself, now to appear in the [very] presence of God on our behalf.

Nor did He [enter into the heavenly sanctuary to] offer Himself regularly again and again, as the high priest enters the [Holy of] Holies every year with blood not his own;

For then would He often have had to suffer, [over and over again] since the foundation of the world. But as it now is, He has once for all at the consummation *and* close of the ages appeared to put away *and* abolish sin by His sacrifice [of Himself].

And just as it is appointed for [all] men once to die and after that the [certain] judgment,

Even so it is that Christ having been offered to take upon Himself *and* bear as a burden the sins of many once *and* once for all, will appear a second time, not carrying any burden of sin *nor* to deal with sin, but to bring to full salvation those who are (eagerly, and constantly and patiently) waiting for *and* expecting Him. (AMP)

These verses tell us that ". . .under the Law, almost everything is purified by means of blood, and without the shedding of blood there is neither release from sin and its guilt nor the remission of the due and merited punishment for sins." This is why Moses and the Law were so important. The Law, with it sacrifices and blood-sanctification rites, put in check the reign of sin and death until the Seed should come.

It is abundantly clear that biblical Israel enjoyed no permanent "release from sin" by the blood of animals.

Israel had to continually offer the blood of animals to atone for sins. There was no other way to be cleansed. The purifying of the people and the "sacred appliances" of the tabernacle was done by sprinkling them with blood. Blood became the cleanser, the purifier, the sanctifier.

God Is A God Of Faith

God did not create man's blood to be shed, though He knew it would be shed. He did not create man to sin, though He knew he would sin. He did not create man to die — unless God is in the business of creating faulty equipment — but He knew that man would flirt with sin and die. God is a God of faith. He gave man a will, the ability to make choices, and by faith He trusted that enough men would ultimately make the right choices.

Being our Creator and all-knowing, God knew that man would sin. He saw the need for blood as a covering for sin and as the remitter of sin, but those were secondary purposes. God did not plan for man to fail, so blood could not have been designed primarily as a fail-safe device.

I believe that God created blood as the carrier of man's physical life as well as a carrier of his spirit life.

The Bible says in Gen. 2:7:

> **And the Lord God formed man *of* the dust of the ground, and breathed into his nostrils the breath of life; and man became a living soul.**

That "breath of life" was blown through Adam's nostrils and into his lungs, and man started to live.

Let me show you how I believe the process of life

came about in man:

Blood makes two circuits in the body. In the first, it is pumped from the heart to the lungs. In the lungs, oxygen breathed in from air attaches itself to hemoglobin molecules in the red blood cells. The blood then returns to the heart. This circuit is called pulmonary circulation.

Blood is then pumped from the heart throughout the body and returns to the heart. This circuit is called systemic circulation.

On the first circuit, when oxygen attaches itself to blood in the lungs, blood becomes a bright red color after taking on oxygen. As it travels throughout the body on the second circuit, the hemoglobin molecules release the oxygen as blood comes in contact with tissue cells in need of a fresh supply of oxygen. Red blood cells then unload their cargo of oxygen and nutrients, and take on the tissue cells' carbon dioxide and other waste. Blood now becomes a lead blue color as it heads back to the heart to make the first circuit again.

In Adam, our representative, it would have worked the same way. Why? Because God is no respecter of persons (Acts 10:34). Adam's breathing process could not have worked any differently than ours.

Breathing In The Breath Of Life

God jump-started life in man by breathing into Adam's nostrils the breath of life. That breath was blown into his lungs. In the Hebrew, the word *breath* is the word *neshamah,* which indicates "vital breath." Several translations identify this as the *soul.* Others identify it as both the soul and/or spirit. The Amplified Bible translates the word *breath* to mean the "spirit of life."

I believe that it is all right for us to say that God

breathed "the spirit of life" into Adam's nostrils. Each molecule of hemoglobin in Adam's blood had God's breath — pure spirit — attached to it. So spirit, or breath, from God caused life in man.

Here's my scenario: That spirit of life was blown into Adam's lungs, where it first manifested with his blood. Blood sprang to life with spirit, and it began to enliven all the cells in the tissue. Spirit-life soaked into the heart and it began to pump, and it continually pumped life-giving blood to every cell of Adam's body. Adam became a living soul. The way I see it, human life, both physically and spiritually, began in the blood.

Now look at what Jesus said in John 6:63: ". . . the words that I speak unto you, *they* are spirit, and *they* are life." This word *spirit* is the word *pneuma* in the Greek. It means breath. It is the same thing that God breathed into Adam's nostrils when he became a living soul. And because what is breathed into the lungs attaches itself to the blood and is carried by the bloodstream, God's breath was coursing through Adam's bloodstream. I believe that the more Adam communed with God, the more his outward glory or covering reflected the spirit that he was breathing in.

This is the same *pneuma* and life that is available to us when we commune with God through the Word. We're breathing in the same *pneuma*. Whatever God's Word is, that same substance makes up spirit and life.

I believe that we can extend our natural life by communing with God through His Word in this same manner. Think about it: by speaking, thinking and meditating God's words — spirit and life — we are communing with God, just as Adam did. So today we can still enjoy some of the privileges that Adam enjoyed, and we can improve the quality of our natural lives in the process.

Life (Spirit) Requires A Physical Carrier

"Life itself is spiritual, but it must have a physical carrier, and this carrier is the blood," writes H.A. Maxwell Whyte in *The Power of the Blood.*

"But, to me, the most amazing thing about blood is its capacity to carry the life of God. The contact between the Divine and the human rests in the bloodstream. No wonder we say that blood is a mysterious substance! It contains something which no scientist can explain. It contains the life of God!"[4]

So Whyte believed also that blood is a point of contact between the human and the Divine.

(Just as an aside, let us return to the role of the red blood cells (or the erythrocytes) and look at a similarity between what the cells do and what Jesus did for us. The red blood cells take life in the form of breath, or fresh oxygen, and nutrients to the tissue cells and in exchange pick up the tissue cells' waste products. Similarly, Jesus took our sins and iniquities. When he took those sins and iniquities, he put them far from us. The body takes those waste products and disposes of them, either through expiration of breath or through bodily waste. Just as the blood delivers fresh oxygen to the cells, He delivered to us His righteousness. He took our sinful waste, but we, as Christians, receive His spiritual life.)

The Scripture tells us that "without shedding of blood is no remission" (Heb. 9:22) and that "the life of the flesh is in the blood" (Lev. 17:11). These verses indicate that blood has a spiritual as well as a physical component. However, the spiritual properties are not as apparent as the physical properties.

One would not ordinarily study the spiritual properties of blood in a biology or anatomy class as they might study blood's physical properties. It would be wonderful if schools taught the spiritual side of our makeup along with the physical side, but they don't — at least, not from a godly point of view. As Trumbull points out in *The Blood Covenant*, the spiritual properties of blood were evident to primitive man from time immemorial. For modern man, the laboratory for studying blood's spiritual properties is the Word of God.

Law: The Law of Sin and Blood

(Where there is sin there must be blood. If there is no sin, there will be no blood.)

Major points:

1. All shed blood is the result of sin.

2. All human blood is tainted because of Adam and Eve's transgression.

3. Sin creates breaches in the spirit world.

4. Adam and Eve gave birth to human sin.

5. Sin must be covered or it will spread.

6. Uncovered sin will result in human bloodshed.

7. Blood is the only covering for sin.

8. Man shows unification with God by eating the sacrifice.

9. Only Jesus' blood had the spiritual power to deliver mankind.

10. Human blood is the carrier of physical and spiritual life.

11. God blew spirit-life into Adam's nostrils; it was picked up and carried by his blood.

TWO

OUR BLOOD COVERING

Most people have no trouble understanding
what the Bible means when it says "the life of
the flesh is in the blood." This makes sense to
the logic in us. It appeals to our reason and our scientific nature. Still, there is a hint of some spiritual truth
that goes beyond any purely scientific truth, because life
itself cannot be explained purely by scientific reasoning.
But most people simply accept this truth either unques-
tioningly or unconsciously, without finding out what it
means.

Our Blood Covering

Taken purely as a physical truth, when we say that the "life of the flesh is in the blood," it means that without the river of life circulating through the body, no cells could receive oxygen and nutrients. Nor could they dispose of their waste. We understand that without these activities in the cells, the organs and the body would simply die.

Most people have no trouble understanding that much, but on the other hand they may ask, "How can blood remit (or put away) sin?" or "How can the blood of Jesus save me?"

These are valid questions. If medical and biological science can explain so well the physical properties of blood, why shouldn't God's people have an equally valid understanding of its spiritual properties? By looking at both the physical and spiritual properties, I believe we should and can have an equally valid explanation.

As to how blood can remit sin, we must remember that blood plays two roles: It is both a physical response and a spiritual response. It is a carrier-sustainer of both physical life and of spiritual life. Obviously, remitting sin requires a spiritual response. Just as blood responds to an infection or a wound in the physical body, it responds to sin (an infection or a wound) in the spirit.

Without becoming too technical, let me explain that blood will do miraculous things to protect the human body. When the body is cut or damaged, three protective processes immediately occur: The blood vessels begin to contract so that blood loss is restricted to the wounded area; next, microscopic blood platelets begin to clump together around the wound, laying the foundation for a clot; lastly, a clot is formed and eventually a scab to cover and further protect the wound. If blood loss is not in massive amounts, these processes will usually be sufficient to halt blood flow through the wound.

If blood loss is in massive amounts, then blood pressure will drop, and nerve impulses will cause a powerful wave of reflexes throughout the body which constrict the blood vessels to slow blood loss. Meanwhile, the heartbeat may climb to more than double its normal rate to keep the remaining blood flowing to vital organs, especially the heart and brain.

Once germs or infection enter the body, microscopic white blood cells (a form of leukocytes) engulf and consume them. Often, there is visible inflammation (pus around the wound) as the battle in the tissue is being fought. When the invading germs have been dispersed, the body begins to heal and recover itself.

Satan: Author Of All Damage To The Body

"We must realize that Satan is the author of all damage to the body," writes H.A. Maxwell Whyte in *The Power of the Blood.* "Demons try to attack any injured part of our body and permit germs, which are always around us, to impinge on the injured flesh and do their work of destruction and poisoning. But when the Blood of Jesus is applied in faith, it acts as a covering which prevents Satan from attacking us with germs. Therefore, the natural healing processes in our body quickly do their work, for they are not hindered by Satan. The Blood of Jesus is the finest covering and disinfectant in the world. It is perfect." [1]

When there is sin prevalent in the life of a believer, the spiritual properties of blood are necessary to cover it. Blood will engulf the sin and disperse it. It will close the wound by "clotting," and put a "scab" or a seal on it so that the healing can take place. It is not our blood, but the blood of Jesus that comes to the rescue. His blood

36

has been made available to cover sins of the past, the present and the future.

The Old Testament word for remitting, or putting away of sin, was the word *atone. Atone* means to cover. The blood of animals was used to atone for or to cover the sins of the people. Once a year, the high priest entered into the Holy of Holies to pour blood upon the mercy seat. The shekinah glory would appear and God would commune with the high priest. Woe unto the high priest who would enter into the Holy of Holies without blood. He would be stricken dead.

We who have received Jesus as our Savior and Lord have been cleansed from sin by His blood. Our sins have been remitted, or sent away from us. Today, the rough equivalent of atonement versus remitting would be like covering a dirty spot on a carpet with a rug or a piece of furniture (atoning) or having the carpet cleaned (remitting).

When we sin, we have only to confess that sin, according to 1 John 1:9, and He is faithful and just to *cleanse* us from all unrighteousness. How is this cleansing done, and with what agent? It is done by the cleansing power of the blood.

So we can now understand that the "life of the flesh is in the blood" and that blood is a remitter of sin. But Romans 6:23 reminds us of another truth. That is, "the wages of sin is death." The logical extension of this concept would be that for every sin there must be a death to pay for it. (Remember the first sin, and then the first animal sacrifice? Or the first sin and the first blood?)

But knowing the mercy and goodness of God, we cannot conceive that the law would be so immediate as to demand a death for every sin, no matter how minor the sin. But it does. For every sin there must be a death.

Or put another way: For every sin there must be blood to cover it, as the Law of Sin and Blood states.

But whose death and whose blood?

The good news is that Jesus paid for our sins, and accepted our wages of death. He has paid for all the sins of mankind. All man needs to do is accept what has already been provided. In other words, there is no more need that any other blood be shed, because the blood of Jesus is enough to cover all sins.

A Sinner Could Not Have Paid For Sin

Our sins against God had to be paid by the blood of someone who was sinless. How could a sinner pay for sin when he had no righteousness? Without righteousness, we cannot even approach God. Because man's blood had been made spiritually worthless, he could not solve this problem of his own making. God's own blood had to be shed for us. God had to prepare a body that could carry sinless blood to redeem mankind.

Col. 1:12-14:

> **Giving thanks unto the Father, which hath made us meet to be partakers of the inheritance of the saints in light:**

> **Who hath delivered us from the power of darkness, and hath translated us into the kingdom of his dear Son:**

> **In whom we have redemption through his blood, even the forgiveness of sins:**

Verse 20:

> **And, having made peace [with us] through**

**the blood of his cross, by him to reconcile
all things unto himself; by him, *I say*,
whether they be things in the earth or
things in heaven.**

God has made peace with us through the reconciliation of Jesus' blood. We are no more strangers, but sons of God. Through His blood we have gained an inheritance of the saints in light. We have been brought back into the status of Adam. Man can now be declared righteous by accepting God's clemency, and can approach unto God.

We can see that all the blood shed up until the crucifixion could not redeem man. Many, many thousands of animals perished, but their blood could never accomplish what the blood of Jesus accomplished. In fact, I believe we can see in this another law, **The Law of Equality in Blood**, which says: *The blood of the redeemer must be equal to the blood of the sinner.*

In other words, the redemptive power in the blood must at least be at a level where it can nullify the destructive power of the sin that was committed. It had to clean both the spirit and the flesh. Not just the flesh, as animal blood could do, but the spirit as well. In Jesus' blood, I believe we have that match. When Jesus died upon that cross, it was as if Adam died 6,000 years later for the transgression he had committed. It took blood that was equal to Adam's blood (or sin) to pay the original debt. With Jesus's death, the debt is paid.

1st Cor. 15:22:

> **For as in Adam all die, even so in Christ
> shall all be made alive.**

The Bible calls Him the last Adam.

1st Cor. 15: 45:

And so it is written, The first man Adam was made a living soul; the last Adam was made a quickening spirit.

To conclude this point, let's go back to Col. 1:14, which says, "In whom we have redemption through his blood, even the forgiveness of sins." So we see we have been liberated from sin's grasp and placed in a new relationship with our Savior.

An Unholy Link

There is an unholy link between sin and death. This fact is supported by Scripture throughout both the Old and New Testaments. Romans 5:12 clearly indicates the impact of these twin devastations in Adam's transgression.

Wherefore, as by one man sin entered into the world, and death by sin; and so death passed upon all men, for that all have sinned:

The more one reads that statement the more one realizes the far-reaching implications of Adam's sin. The man who allowed sin to come into the world, also allowed death, which includes bloodshed, to come in. Death is a characteristic of sin. What Adam did affected all men from the Garden until when the Lord Jesus returns to set up His Kingdom. Death — that is, spiritual death, or estrangement from Almighty God — was allowed to come upon all men.

We cannot say that physical death is always an immediate result of sin. It is clear that it is not. The Bible tells us that Adam lived another 800 years after Seth, and "begat sons and daughters." So Eve apparently bore more offspring than Cain, Abel, and Seth. Cain and Seth probably took their own sisters as wives, since they would have had no other choices in selecting spouses, and continued to populate the earth. We do not know how many children Adam and Eve had, but they lived a lot longer than anyone we have known during our times, so it could have been a very great number by our standards today.

Though Adam lived several hundred years after being cast from the Garden, physical death was working in him. Finally, at the great age of 930, he passed from the scene. We can deduce from this that physical death follows spiritual death. The fact that it took so long for Adam to die physically points to either the remarkable survival qualities of the human body, which God never intended to die, or to the fact that men of that time still lived in a purer world with a purer knowledge of God handed down from Adam. Or, perhaps, a combination of both.

No Physical Pollution Of The World

The world then was not polluted as ours is today. There were no factories to foul the rivers and streams. There were no cars and industries to pollute the air. These factors alone would make a massive difference in the two environments. Sin had not completed it's physical takeover.

God, being perfect, did not create flawed humans. That would have been another form of pollution. Everything God created was "good," though not incorruptible. Since there is no death in God, He could not put

41

death in man. That would not have been "good." Death was an alien concept to Adam. He had to learn to die. It was not something that God had built into him.

Before his transgression, Adam enjoyed constant Face-to-face communion with the Creator of all the universe. He walked and talked with God in the Garden. The more he communed with God, the stronger his spiritual covering became. That covering — that glory — was in evidence all around him. After the act of original sin, this communion was broken, the glory covering lifted and, as a consequence, both Adam and Eve died spiritually.

Without their glory covering, Adam and Eve's nakedness was revealed. They could see the contrast between what they had been and what they now were. They were wretched and "unclothed." Sin covered them, affecting everything they did, saw, heard, tasted, touched and said. Their perceptions changed; It was as if they were forced to live within a bubble of dirty cellophane. Nothing seemed real to them anymore.

Now they realized what God meant when He warned them not to eat of the tree of the knowledge of good and evil. They had lost their innocence, and it showed, because their glory was gone. One had to wear glory clothes in the Garden. Because they did not have the proper attire, so to speak, an angel ushered them out of the Garden in shame. They could not stay in the Garden without their glory suits.

Adam, the first man and representative of all men that were to follow, forfeited Face-to-face communion with God for himself and for all men. This was the type of communion where Adam could sit down, look God in the eye and chat, or play, or have dinner with Him. He could grab God and hug Him. Adam could laugh and talk with his Creator, or even play games and joke. It must have been wonderful. It most have been joy unspeakable, and they had all of eternity to be together. Adam literally could become lost in God's never-ending love, which he probably did. He got drunk on love. God could smother him with the warmth of His glory. Adam learned from the Father how all the spiritual principles worked, and everything he saw God do, he did — like father, like son.

That kind of life was a privilege that all Adam's descendants should have enjoyed as a spiritual right, but Adam gave that privilege away. That communion remained broken until Jesus came to restore man to his proper position of righteousness.

The point in all this is that the wages of sin is death. Sin cut us off from God. The moment Adam sinned, his spirit died and the glory took flight. Adam's spirit was a reflection of his relationship with God. He was on his way to perfection, but lost it.

God Cannot Look Upon Sin

We know that God cannot look upon sin. Habakkuk 1:13 says: "Thou art of purer eyes than to behold evil, and canst not look upon iniquity..." God and sin cannot agree, and because of that, sin must be put away from Him. The lesson in Romans 6:23, which says that the wages of sin is death, lies in the idea that each sin we commit pushes us farther away from God, the source of all life, because it draws us closer to death. Each sin we commit opens the breach wider. That sin must be covered by blood and the breach closed if we are to continue living under God's protection. Otherwise, the uncovered sin itself draws more sin and eventually causes destruction to overtake us.

God cannot be where sin is exalted. When Adam's spirit died, God could no longer commune with him Face to face. Life, which was manifested in Adam's glory and spirit, again took up residence in the blood, where it started out when God first breathed life into his nostrils.

Man, being cut off spiritually, or spiritually dead, had no choice but to live out his existence outside of fellowship with Almighty God. But God was not willing to give up on his highest creation. (He is not willing that any should perish.) Man had botched Plan A, so God instituted Plan B. Plan B, like Plan A, involved blood. But now it was not blood on the inside, as a launching pad for the spirit; It was blood on the outside as a covering for sin. The only way man could close the spiritual breach between himself and God was through blood, though not man's own. God could commune with Adam if his sin was covered with blood. In fact, it was the *only* way he could commune with him.

Gen. 3:8-9:

> **And they heard the voice of the Lord God walking in the garden in the cool of the day: and Adam and his wife hid themselves from the presence of the Lord God amongst the trees of the garden.**
>
> **And the Lord God called unto Adam, and said unto him, Where art thou?**

Is there anyone who believes that God Almighty, the all-seeing, all-knowing one, really had to ask Adam where he was? I don't think so. God knew precisely where Adam and Eve were hiding. So why did God not appear to them as He had in the past.

I believe the reason Adam and Eve "heard *the voice* of the Lord God walking in the garden in the cool of the day," but did not see His presence, is because God Himself could not confront Adam or look Face to face upon them without destroying them. Adam's nature had changed. He now represented sin, not his Father God. He had changed families. God, we have pointed out, cannot look upon sin.

Verse 8 also says, "and Adam and his wife hid themselves from the presence of the Lord God..." Notice what it does *not* say: It does not say that God's presence *was* in the Garden, but that Adam and Eve hid themselves from the *presence* of the Lord God. I believe Adam and Eve hid themselves from what they *believed* was the presence of the Lord God. They believed it was the presence of the Lord God because they heard His voice walking in the Garden in the cool of the day. Since Adam, godly men have had to become accustomed to hearing God's voice but not seeing His presence.

Had Adam not sinned, he would have remained sensitive enough to know where God was. But his spirit had died. Adam now had become truly blind. He could only see what was in the physical world; he could no longer see in the spirit world.

God was Adam's Creator; he was used to constant fellowship with Him. But God could no longer put His presence in the Garden because the Garden was now a place of sin, and God cannot be in manifestation where sin is. Adam's spirit was dead. I don't believe God could even appear in a vision to a dead spirit. There was nothing left of Adam for God to fellowship with, other than flesh, and God cannot fellowship with flesh because His presence will destroy it. God's presence would have also destroyed the Garden and everything in it.

Giving Adam Security With His Voice

So God used His voice as a ventriloquist might use his, by "throwing" it from His presence, or "walking it," as if He were actually in the Garden looking for Adam. God in His infinite mercy did this to give Adam security, to assure him that He had not left him.

I believe that Adam would have died from sheer panic if God had not continued to talk with him in the Garden. Here Adam was, in a very unfamiliar, sinful state, locked out of the spirit world, a world that had been as much a part of his life as the physical world. In fact, they were inseparable to him. He did not know where one began and the other ended. Had he not eaten of the tree of the knowledge of good and evil, he would have never known the separation of the one world from the other.

Adam felt alone, cold, fearful, mistrustful; even the Garden seemed unfamiliar. Eve herself seemed different, almost a stranger. In just the short span of time since their glory had lifted, Adam was shocked at how Eve's body had begun to change. His was changing too. The luster was gone. There were lines in his face and spots he had never seen. He felt pain. He had accidents now, falls, and he made mistakes, something he had never done before he sinned. Sin had turned his world upside-down. He needed to hear from God; he needed some kind of assurance.

But I believe God's presence was, in fact, not there, and only His voice was there to comfort Adam until such time as the gravity of his condition sank in. Adam needed to prepare for a very different kind of life outside the

Garden. He needed time to learn to how to cope in a world without constant communion with his Creator. He needed time to adjust, and I am sure God was very generous with him. But slowly, over a period of time, the voice grew fainter, and Adam began to realize he would see God's face no more on the earth.

It Had To Be Innocent Blood

So not just any blood could atone for man's sin. It had to be spiritually innocent blood, and as the Law of Equality in Blood states: To redeem man it had to be blood on the same level as the sinner's.

The Bible tells us that Abel, a righteous man, was the first man to die physically. But not even Abel's blood would have worked as a sacrifice. Abel's blood was in the same condition as Cain's. Abel was counted as a righteous man because he was diligent to cover his sins with blood, but Abel's blood cried out for vengeance, just as any other man's blood would have. Vengeance would not have helped man; it was mercy that was needed. And there is no reason to believe that any other man's blood would have been more compassionate than Abel's. If you look at Revelation 6: 9-10 you will see why I can make such a statement:

> **And when he had opened the fifth seal, I saw under the altar the souls of them that were slain for the word of God, and for the testimony which they held:**

> **And they cried with a loud voice, saying, How long, O Lord, holy and true, dost thou not judge and *avenge* our blood on them that dwell on the earth?**

47

Even the blood of these men "slain for the word of God" is seeking vengeance. I don't believe it was possible for any man in his fallen state to have been any more compassionate than Abel. That is why animals were used. No bull, ram, lamb, or goat had ever sinned, nor did these animals have any consciousness of sin, though they lived in the same sin-sick world.

These animals had no desire for vengeance against man. They were totally innocent. Their blood may not have betokened mercy, but it did not speak vengeance either. It could thus qualify as atoning blood to be used as a covering for sin. Only innocent blood could satisfy the demands of divine justice, and preserve God's ultimate creation.

But there was another problem. Animal blood is limited in its abilities. For one thing, it could not speak of mercy, and man was in need of mercy. And animal blood was different physically. Even science tells us that. Animal blood does not have the same wonderful array of germ-fighting deterrents as man's blood. Animal blood could never attain the same spiritual potency that man's blood could attain through devotion to God, because animals do not have spirits. Their blood could never stand against sin the way that an innocent man's could. Nor was animal's blood as precious to God as human blood. Animal blood was simply the best that could be offered at the time. Animal's blood was only good for the outside, not the inside.

God has never required man to sacrifice his or another man's life, although human sacrifice later became widely practiced throughout the world. What would the sacrifice of a man have accomplished? No man's blood was innocent, since all men had Adam's sin nature. Man was conscious of sin. Though blood was the covering for sin, no man's blood could cover the sins of man. His death as a sacrifice would have been meaningless.

Beside that, human sacrifice was something that God abhorred. It was a waste of human life. His patience grew short with nations that practiced human sacrifice, though I believe many, if not all, did it at first in ignorance. God knew better than anyone that the blood of man was unsuitable to be offered up. God knew when He planned the universe that man would sin and need to make blood sacrifices, so he provided animals for that purpose.

Thanks be to God that the Creator only once accepted the sacrifice of human life — a final sacrifice — that being the life of His only begotten son, Jesus Christ, who came for the express purpose of redeeming man. But even Jesus was a volunteer. It was His choice. God the Father did not compel Him.

In Hebrews 10:5-7, we find these important words:

> **Wherefore when he cometh into the world, he saith, Sacrifice and offering thou wouldest not, but a body hast thou prepared me:**

> **In burnt offering and sacrifices for sin thou hast had no pleasure.**

> **Then said I, Lo, I come (in the volume of the book it is written of me,) to do thy will, O God.**

Law of Equality in Blood:

(The blood of the redeemer must be equal to blood of the sinner.)

Major points:

1. Where there is sin in a believer's life, Jesus' blood will cover it.

2. Jesus' blood engulfs sin and disperses it.

3. Every sin must have blood to cover it.

4. Jesus' blood covers all sins.

5. When Adam's spirit died, life again took up residence in his blood.

6. God could not commune with Adam Face to face after he sinned.

7. Man's death as a sacrifice would have been a waste of life.

THREE

DEFILEMENT VS. SANCTIFICATION

Then what is the relationship between blood and sin? — remembering, of course, that sin represents death. We can only reason from what we know about the relationship between blood and life. We know that Adam had life flowing in his blood because God had breathed the "breath of life" into him. That breath in his lungs was picked up by his blood and transferred to all the cells throughout his body. His body was then made alive.

The Amplified Bible refers to this breath as "the spirit of life," so I believe we are justified in saying that Adam had spirit-life flowing in his blood. Adam nurtured this spirit-life by communing with the Word of Life, or God Himself. He communed with God daily, Face to face. The spirit-life in his blood developed into an outward manifestation or covering, which was his glory covering.

Adam clearly was the god of this world, and he fellowshipped daily with the God of the Universe. Adam had dominion over all the Garden. His mind was unlimited; He named all the animals. What he saw God do, He did.

God had put him in charge. He had a position that Satan always wanted; he had the body that would make him god of the physical world that Satan always wanted. Adam was a child of both the spirit and the physical worlds. Satan could see the manifestation of Adam's spirit in the glory that surrounded him. He detested Adam and formed a plan to nullify him. Satan set out to bring about Adam's downfall, by using the only trick he has ever had — deceit.

Thus blood, the carrier of spirit and life, was automatically an enemy of Satan. Satan is only interested in death, not in life. If he could defile Adam's blood spiritually through sin, he could defile it physically through disease. He wanted to separate blood from the life that is in it, and he would do it by any means at his disposal.

Satan's effort to get at the blood was through getting Adam to commit an act contrary to the revealed Word of God. He didn't go directly at Adam. He came through Eve. Once he had deceived Eve by getting her to question God's Word, which was law, Adam was an easier mark. Adam, a god-man who had wisdom, total authority and knew better, sided with his wife, Eve, rather than with his

God. In doing so, he committed spiritual suicide. His spirit died, his glory covering fled, and now he and all mankind were open to the devastation of sin.

So Satan accomplished what he had set out to accomplish. That is, he cut man off spiritually from the source of life, which is God, by defiling man's blood through sin.

Satan Took The Form Of A Snake

It is interesting to note that Satan appeared to Eve in the form of a serpent. The Hebrew word for serpent is *nachash*, which means snake. According to *Strong's Exhaustive Concordance of the Bible, nachash* comes from a primary root word of the same spelling but slightly different pronunciation that means to hiss, i.e. whisper, a prognostication, a divine enchanter. Evil purposes are often established in whispers, out of the earshot of everyone else.

Satan was snakishly subtle; he pulled Eve aside, away from Adam and enchanted her as a sorcerer would do. The Bible says in Genesis 3:6, "And *when* the woman saw that the tree was good for food..." To me, that implies there could have been a lapse of time between seeing and acting. "*When the woman saw...*" could mean that she did not see immediately, as it might mean if one said, "*The woman saw* ..." Satan had been working on her mind, preparing her to sin. He enchanted her with the prospects of the future, of something better, something more exotic. But what happens after you're enchanted? You're set up, ready for the kill. The enchanter can then have his way with you.

Some snakes are enchanters. They mesmerize their prey before they strike. Once they strike, the venom works immediately, and it's usually a matter of minutes before they swallow their victims whole. It is very interesting that one of the primary ways a snake's venom kills is by attacking and quickly destroying the blood's corpuscles. Some venoms can render blood unable to clot, while other venoms cause abnormally rapid clotting. Satan had defiled Adam and Eve's blood with the venom of sin, and it would eventually end in death.

Interesting also is the fact that some snakes are constrictors. They crush the life (breath) out of you.

The Nature Of Defilement

Defilement is a spiritual transaction, but it requires a physical act. There can be no defilement if a sin is not committed. A sinful thought that is never acted on dies unborn. Remember Jesus' words when the Pharisees and scribes asked him why his disciples ate food with dirty (or defiled) hands? After he reproved them, Jesus told them, in Mark 7:15, that it is not what a man eats that defiles him, but what comes out of him. In other words, food cannot defile a man, but what a man says and does defiles him.

Now consider what happened to Adam and Eve when they ate of the tree. Their eating itself was a sin because it was a direct violation of God's law. Genesis 2:17 says, "But of the tree of the knowledge of good an evil, thou shalt not eat of it: for in the day that thou eatest thereof thou shalt surely die." After they sinned, they began to take on some of Satan's characteristics. They hid from God, and began passing the blame when God questioned them. Both these are forms of deception, which is Satan's method of operation.

Adam's blood became defiled when he broke God's

54

law. He died immediately spiritually. Although his blood was still effective on a physical plane in that life was still flowing through his flesh, it was not spirit-life. His blood was no longer effective spiritually. His covering was gone. He became spiritually dead, and his physical life was soon to die as well.

Everything in God's creation produces after its own kind. Basset hounds produce basset hounds; robins produce robins, and king cobras produce king cobras. Robins will not produce blackbirds, and king cobras do not produce king snakes. Spiritually dead people cannot produce spiritually alive people.

The same spiritual death that changed Adam and Eve's nature and cut them off from God was passed down from them to all men. Therefore, they could not help but produce people with the same sinful nature they had. This was the worst result of man's fall from grace. He began producing an endless line of flawed people who came from the factory, so to speak, with a nature of sin.

Man's Life Was Meant To Be Forever

God created man to exist forever. It was never intended that man should die. But the fact of Adam's transgression is that this spiritual death passed upon all men. And because all men have inherited spiritual death, they have all inherited physical death, since physical death is a result of spiritual death. This physical death is a reality that all men must face.

Sin and death are all around us because of Adam's transgression — in the air we breathe, in the food we eat, in what we drink, in our neighborhoods, in our schools, on our streets, in what we see, in what we read, and throughout the atmosphere. Germs, which are a result of sin, float around us every day, and the air is filled with pollutants of various kinds. All this is a result of sin.

Here is a Scripture most of us never associate with the air we breathe, but it shows clearly why the air is so bad:

Eph.2:2:

Wherein in time past ye walked according to the course of this world, according to the prince of the power of the air, the spirit that now worketh in the children of disobedience:

Before Christ, we acted as the world acts; we did what the world does, and the world is acting in accordance with the rules of the prince of the power of the air. Who is the prince of the power of the air? It is Satan. So then, life may be in the blood, but death is in the air, and air is a substance the body needs for life. Now, do you see what Adam unleashed into the world? The very air that we are so dependent on to keep breath in our lungs and revitalize our blood is under the control of Satan. What would our lives be like if every breath we took was like Adam's before he sinned — charged with the life of God rather than sin? How much longer would these bodies last if they were not exposed to such a high level of corruption? I believe we could go on forever, and that is exactly what our Father intended.

It is through His breath that God was able to jumpstart life in Adam. Now, with every act of breathing, we draw in pollutants, both physically and spiritually. Even the ozone layer around the earth has been corrupted, and through the air man now sends radio and television, as well as microwave, signals that are as often as not bent on sinful purposes.

Still, very few people, other than environmentalists, talk about the air. But Christians should be talking about it more than others because it is under the control of Satan. Unfortunately, Christians see it as an environmental issue and not part of man's spiritual defilement, but it is. So Adam let an evil genie out of the bottle, and man can't put him back in again. Until Jesus returns, none of us will escape the ravages of physical death, but we can slow them down through the Word and the Blood.

Sin Will Defile Blood

It should not be difficult now to believe that sin can defile blood. Just look at it logically: If sin could not defile blood, then Adam's blood would not have been defiled and man's blood would not be defiled today. Adam's sin would have been without meaning, like eating with unwashed hands. If sin could not defile blood, why use the blood of innocent animals to cover sins? If sin could not defile blood, any man's blood could have remitted sin, and any man's blood could have redeemed mankind. Man would not need a savior, and we would not need to call on the blood of Jesus to cover our sins.

So apparently sin can defile blood.

If the body is diseased, then the blood reflects that condition. The blood cannot be any healthier than the body in which it flows. The blood in a body that has been tainted by disease is not blood that you want transfused into your own body. It would simply spread the disease to you. You don't want to be around that kind of blood because it is deadly. When doctors and nurses are dealing with patients with highly communicable diseases, they handle them with extreme care. They have to protect themselves as well as other patients from contamination.

You would want to dispose of the blood of someone with a highly communicable disease. By the same token, if the body is defiled by sin, then the blood is defiled spiritually by the sin, and cannot be useful for spiritual purposes.

Here is a principle that Jesus enunciated in Matthew 23:16-22 that I believe we can apply to blood:

> **Woe unto you, ye blind guides, which say, Whosoever shall swear by the temple, it is nothing; but whosoever shall swear by the gold of the temple, he is a debtor!**
>
> **Ye fools and blind: for whether is greater, the gold, or the temple that sanctifieth the gold?**
>
> **And, Whosoever shall swear by the altar, it is nothing; but whosoever sweareth by the gift that is upon it, he is guilty.**
>
> **Ye fools and blind: for whether is greater, the gift, or the altar that sanctifieth the gift?**
>
> **Whoso therefore shall swear by the altar, sweareth by it, and by all things thereon.**
>
> **And whoso shall swear by the temple, sweareth by it, and by him that dwelleth therein.**
>
> **And he that shall swear by heaven, sweareth by the throne of God, and by him that sitteth thereon.**

If the gold in the temple is sanctified by the temple, then the same principle must work in our bodies, which are temples of God. The blood in our bodies must be sanctified by our bodies since it is part of our bodies, and our bodies are to be used as instruments of good. By the same token, when our bodies are defiled then the blood in our bodies is defiled. Adam's act defiled his own blood first, and then all men's blood since he passed his tainted bloodline down to all men.

To sanctify means to purify or make ceremonially clean. This is what the sprinkling of blood was all about under the Old Covenant. The priest sanctified the people by sprinkling them with the blood of bulls and goats. We as Christians are made ceremonially clean when we come into the Body of Christ. We are sprinkled, or sanctified, with the blood of Jesus. Sprinkling was an act of faith on the part of the Old Testament people because the priests could not have physically sprinkled all the people. It was done in a symbolic manner. It is the same today. When we come to Jesus, we must come to the sprinkling by faith. No natural blood is going to fall on us.

Heb. 13:12:

> **Wherefore Jesus also, that he might sanctify the people with his own blood, suffered without the gate.**

What this verse is explaining is that Jesus gave His life (shed His blood) outside the walls of the holy city, Jerusalem, just as the animals that were offered as a sacrifice were killed outside the tabernacle. Those who are willing to come out of the city (to come out of sin by coming to Jesus) "bearing His reproach" and acknowledge what He did at the cross, they will be sanctified by faith with the sprinkling of His blood. We need to go back to Hebrews and focus attention on a few verses to support what we are saying here.

Heb. 9:11-14:

> **But Christ being come an high priest of good things to come, by a greater and more perfect tabernacle, not made with hands, that is to say, not of this building;**

> **Neither by the blood of goats and calves, but by his own blood he entered in once into the holy place, having obtained eternal redemption for us.**

> **For if the blood of bulls and of goats, and the ashes of an heifer sprinkling the unclean, sanctifieth to the purifying of the flesh:**

> **How much more shall the blood of Christ, who through the eternal Spirit offered himself without spot to God, purge your conscience from dead works to serve the living God?**

We can see that by faith the blood of animals could sanctify the flesh, but faith in the blood of Jesus goes beyond that. It even sanctifies the conscience and redeems us from our consciousness of guilt and sin. Now look at Hebrews 2:11:

> **For both he that sanctifieth and they who are sanctified are all of one: for which**

60

**cause he is not ashamed to call them breth-
ren.**

The sprinkling of blood brings sanctification, and
through sanctification with His blood we achieve unification with Christ. Now we can see another law established in the Scripture, and that is **The Law of Unification in Blood:** *Faith in the blood (or sanctification by the
blood) brings oneness or unification with Him.* Defilement
destroys unification.

The Making Of A Curse

Before conquering Jericho, Joshua had warned the
people to "in any wise keep yourselves from the accursed
thing, lest *ye make yourselves accursed,* when ye take of the
accursed thing, and make the camp of Israel a curse,
and trouble it" (Josh. 6: 18). The "accursed thing" was
any item dedicated or consecrated to the service of idols.
God told Joshua that Jericho and everything in it was
accursed. Only Rahab, the prostitute who had helped
Israel's spies, and those that were in her house during
the invasion were to be saved.

Like Sodom and Gomorrah before it, Jericho had
reached such a level of defilement that every living thing
in it had to be destroyed. So great was the defilement,
which indicates moral contamination or pollution, that
even the animals were to be destroyed. However, the
children of Israel were allowed to take all the silver, gold
and vessels of brass and iron that they could find.

You will recall how the children of Israel marched
around Jericho for seven days before shouting and making a great ruckus. You remember that the walls of that
great city fell down. What followed was a stunning vic-

tory where Israel captured the city and destroyed all the people, but Rahab's house was saved.

Next, Israel confronted the tiny city of A'i. Spies confidently reported to Joshua that only two or three thousand men were needed to take A'i, certainly not the whole army. But something terrible happened. The small military contingent met with an embarrassing defeat. Thirty-six men were killed — remember the first law, blood for sin — and all the others were chased back to Israel's camp. The people were so devastated by the defeat that their hearts "melted, and became as water" (Josh. 7:5).

Joshua was distraught. He fell on his face before the Lord to find out what caused such a rout. The answer, he found, was sin.

Verse 10-11:

> **And the Lord said unto Joshua, Get thee up; wherefore liest thou thus upon thy face?**

> **Israel hath sinned, and they have also transgressed my covenant which I commanded them: for they have even taken of the accursed thing, and have also stolen, and dissembled also, and they have put it even among their own stuff.**

One man had defied God. ". . . Achan, the son of Carmi, the son of Zabdi, the son of Zerah, of the tribe of Judah, took of the accursed thing: and the anger of the Lord was kindled against the children of Israel" (Josh. 7:1). Achan had stolen items devoted to idol worship and had brought them into Israel's camp. This sinful act defiled the whole nation. Unity with God was broken, and it brought about Israel's defeat, including the death of 36 men.

Because of one man's transgression, the whole nation had sinned and Israel was defeated in a battle that should have amounted to only a skirmish. Only after Achan and "his sons, and daughters, his oxen, his asses, and his sheep" were stoned — more blood for sin — and their bodies burned, along with the accursed items he had taken, could the nation of Israel move forward. Unity with God was re-established. The people's faith and confidence was restored again, and their hearts were no longer "melted as water."

Devastating Impact Of Defilement

Again, Romans 5:12 is the best illustration of how devastating the impact of defilement by sin is:

> **Wherefore, as by one man sin entered into the world, and death by sin; and so death passed upon all men, for that all have sinned:**

One man opened the door to sin in the world and contaminated life for all his descendants. Because of Adam's transgression, all mankind became sinners and fell short of the glory that Adam had achieved, that he wore as a covering at the beginning. That was why Achan's death was necessary. It was not because God is such a hard person that He will not suffer His laws to be broken. That was not the point. The point was: if Achan had remained alive, the whole camp would have been destroyed because of the defilement, and none would have made it to the Promised Land.

I believe that sin and death were passed down to

Adam's progeny through the spiritual defilement of the body and the blood, though physical life remained in the blood. So if life normally resides in the blood, there is great reason to believe that sin and death are retained in the flesh. The corruption of sin has taken up residence in our physical bodies and will reside there until our bodies are redeemed. Look at what Paul says in his letter to the Romans.

Rom. 7:14-25:

> **For we know that the law is spiritual: but I am carnal, sold under sin.**
>
> **For that which I do I allow not: for what I would, that I do not; but what I hate, that do I.**
>
> **If then I do that which I would not, I consent unto the law that it is good.**
>
> **Now then it is no more I that do it, but sin that dwelleth in me.**
>
> *For I know that in me* **(that is, in my flesh),** *dwelleth no good thing:* **for to will is present with me; but how to perform that which is good I find not.**
>
> **For the good that I would I do not: but the evil which I would not, that I do.**
>
> **Now if I do that I would not, it is no more I that do it, but sin that dwelleth in me.**
>
> **I find then a law, that, when I would do good, evil is present with me.**

For I delight in the law of God after the inward man:

But I see another law in my members, warring against the law of my mind, and bringing me into captivity to the law of sin which is in my members.

O wretched man that I am! who shall deliver me from the body of this death?

I thank God through Jesus Christ our Lord. So then with the mind I myself serve the law of God; but with the flesh the law of sin.

God has always been so zealous that His people not be defiled that He did not allow them, especially the priests, to touch the dead or to come in contact with people with running sores, leprosy or other diseases. Nor were they to eat certain kinds of animal flesh, such as the flesh of animals that eat carrion (or dead and putrefying flesh). And they could never eat blood because of the life that it carried. God wanted a holy, sanctified people, a people with whom He could commune on a regular basis.

God wants us undefiled by the things of the world.

If you're not convinced by now that blood can be defiled, let me ask one question.

What set Jesus apart other than the fact that He lived a life so that His blood was undefiled?

Law of Unification in Blood:

(Faith in the blood of Jesus brings about sanctification and unification.)

Major points:

1. Blood is an enemy of Satan.

2. Defilement is spiritual, but it requires a physical act.

3. Defilement comes through sin.

4. Blood is defiled because of sin.

5. After sin, Adam and Eve began to take on Satan's characteristics — the results of defilement.

6. The environment is defiled by sin.

7. Jesus' blood sanctifies us.

8. Flesh is defiled because of sin

FOUR

THE LIVING BLOOD

One morning as I was praising God during my devotion, a song came to mind that many have probably sung at church. The song is such a simple, catchy tune, that it stays with you long after you have stopped singing. The words go like this:

> *I know it was the Blood;*
> *I know it was the Blood;*
> *I know it was the Blood for me.*
> *One day when I was lost,*

HOW THE BLOOD WORKS

He died upon the cross;
I know it was the Blood for me.

As I sang this song over several times, I of course repeated the refrain about "one day when I was lost, He died upon the cross." About the third or fourth time I repeated "He died upon the cross," I heard a small voice say inside me, "Yes, but my blood didn't die."

I can't tell you what that did to my devotion. I was on a joyous high, singing, laughing and praising God because of this revelation. Another piece of the puzzle to understanding the blood had fallen into place.

Thank God that Jesus' blood never died. If it had, it would have been curtains for us. That blood is still alive and, I believe, just as potent as it ever was. I believe that blood is doing in the Body of Christ what human blood does in our individual bodies. It is bringing life; it is hauling away our refuse; it is nourishing all the bands and joints.

Part of the mystery of human blood is that given the right conditions, it can stay alive for several weeks outside of the body. But the body cannot stay alive very long without the blood. When a donor gives blood under correct medical procedures, it can then be stored and kept for weeks, although it must be refrigerated. Because of this ability of blood to stay alive, medicine has been able to save innumerable lives. This allows blood, the fluid of life, to be available for use in operations and transfusions. Isn't that a wonderful saving feature that The Creator has built into our blood? Blood saves; it keeps the body alive.

Jesus' blood is so pure and free from taint that it can exist eternally — without refrigeration.

Here is a revelation that the Lord gave me as I meditated on the purity of His blood: What is truly pure and alive cannot die, because what is pure cannot contain any adulterated things that can kill it. It is beyond the scope of this book to prove this other than to point to the Blood itself, but I believe it to be true. So let's establish another law: **The Law of Purity in Blood:** *Jesus' blood, like His Word, is pure. What is pure cannot die, but exists forever.*

Since what is truly pure must exist forever, it can never be exhausted. It is limitless. Like God Himself, it exists outside of time. Therefore, time has no relevance in relation to His blood. True purity must be able to exist outside of time. True purity is eternal. No matter how many times you sprinkle the Blood and no matter how many people you sprinkle with it, it can never run out or grow weak. No matter how many people are washed in the Blood, there is always enough to cleanse all the others. No matter how many times we call on the Blood, it will always be available. This is the Blood that covers us.

Why What Is Pure Cannot Be Exhausted

At the risk of becoming too technical, I want to try to explain why a pure thing can never be used up or exhausted. I believe the Lord shared this with me as I was contemplating the subject of the purity of His blood. A pure thing can never be used up because it is never using its essence to affect other things.

Let me put it this way: If I have $100,000 and I put that $100,000 in, say, an annuity that pays me the interest on my money every month, I am not touching the essence when I receive my monthly interest-only check. I am simply being blessed by a residual benefit. The essence, the $100,000, remains. It goes on in perpetuity.

Here is another example: Our Earth orbits the sun. The sun's warmth and light keeps us alive. It keeps the planet from freezing, its light helps plants grow, and its rays provide other useful benefits. If a man decided he wanted to get closer to the sun's essence, he would probably use a spaceship. Somewhere between Earth and Venus, where the temperatures range around 800 degrees Fahrenheit, he would begin to realize what a foolish move he had made. He could not stand the heat.

Man in his present state cannot take essence, but he can exist very well off the residual benefits. The essence kills, until we are changed into another form: spirit. The blood, like the sun, is enough for everyone on the planet, because it cannot be exhausted. There is no nation that exists in darkness. There is enough sun for all. And, also, there is enough Son for all. Indeed, the sun, our great star, will someday burn itself out, but the Son will forever shine brightly, and His blood will never lose its power. So man must be washed and sprinkled with the Blood by faith, not by blood itself.

Jesus never sinned, so there was no defilement in his blood. His blood is perfect, not merely innocent. He achieved perfection by the sinless life He lived on earth. It is the defilement of sin that brings death, but death never had a claim on Jesus. Jesus could have never even told a "little white lie" or even given a false impression. If he had, the taint of sin would have been on Him. And now no sin can ever get to the Blood. First, because there is no sin in heaven to defile it and second, because no sin can stand the essence. Indeed, there is an indication that Jesus' blood was necessary to purify things in heaven. Rebellion against God had reached that far. Hebrews 9:22-24 gives us some insight into the effect of sin's penetration into heaven.

> **And almost all things are by the law purged with blood; and without shedding of blood is no remission.**

It was therefore necessary that the patterns of things in the heavens should be purified with these [that is, the sacrifices of calves and goats]**; but the heavenly things themselves with better sacrifices than these.**

For Christ is not entered into the holy places made with hands, which are the figures of the true; but into heaven itself, now to appear in the presence of God for us:

Jesus' blood is not sprinkled in any earthly tabernacle, but in heaven. The heavenly things required a better blood than the blood of mere animals, and of mere men. The heavenly things are not shadows and types, as things are in the earth. They are the real things, the true things. They had to be sanctified with pure blood, and it had to be from someone who would dare to go beyond what any other man had done in terms of living a holy, obedient and undefiled life.

Heb. 9:25-26:

Nor yet that he should offer himself often, as the high priest entereth into the holy place every year with blood of others;

For then must he often have suffered since the foundation of the world: but now once in the end of the world hath he appeared to put away sin by the sacrifice of himself.

Jesus only had to offer His blood once. That sanctifying act was final. He is not like the earthly high priests, who had to offer sacrifices every year for the sins of the people. So we can see another law, unprovable except by faith, **The Law of Sanctification in Blood:** *Earthly acts of*

71

sanctification can never be permanently established in the earth, but heavenly acts of sanctification are permanently established both in heaven and earth.

What Jesus established cannot be changed. It is established forever. He is a God that changes not.

Why Did Jesus' Body Die?

But if Jesus' blood didn't die, how is it that His body did? It died because of the suffering and torture it had to endure on earth. It was a human body.

According to a March 21, 1986, Special Report entitled "On the Physical Death of Jesus Christ" in the Journal of the American Medical Association, Jesus was probably near death when he was crucified.

> "The severe scourging, with its intense pain and appreciable blood loss, most probably left Jesus in a preshock state. Moreover, hematidrosis [bloody sweat] had rendered his skin particularly tender. The physical and mental abuse meted out by the Jews and the Romans, as well as the lack of food, water, and sleep, also contributed to his generally weakened state. Therefore, even before the actual crucifixion, Jesus' physical condition was at least serious and possibly critical...."

> "Although the Romans did not invent crucifixion, they perfected it as a form of torture and capital punishment that was designed to produce a slow death with maximum pain and suffering. It was one of the most disgraceful and cruel methods of execution and usually was reserved only for

slaves, foreigners, revolutionaries and the
vilest of criminals."

According to the report, it was customary for the
condemned man to carry his own cross, or at least the
crossbar, since the whole cross usually weighed well over
300 pounds. Further humiliation was heaped on the vic-
tim by making him carry the cross naked. Along the way
and throughout the crucifixion, he had to endure the
taunting and jeers of both the soldiers and the crowds.
At the crucifixion site, tapered iron nails 5 to 7 inches in
length were pounded through his wrist and feet.

Insects burrowed "into the wounds or the eyes, ears
and nose ... and birds of prey would tear at these sites.
Moreover, it was customary to leave the corpse on the
cross to be devoured by predatory animals." To hurry
death, guards would break the victims' legs. To make
certain of death, they "would pierce the body with a sword
or lance. Traditionally, this had been considered a spear
wound to the heart through the right side of the chest
— a fatal wound probably taught to most Roman soldiers." Out of the wound flowed blood and water.

The report points out the medical aspects of crucifixion, revealing in painful detail the agony that each
affected portion of the body was subjected to, and the
breakdown of the body's proper function. "Death by crucifixion was, in every sense of the word, excruciating."[1]

The Blood Was Poured Out

Jesus' blood was shed both before and after crucifixion. Shed means to *spill forth; to expend; to pour out.*
That blood had to be pure on earth to be considered
pure in heaven, though Jesus still had to finish His course
and His blood be offered up in the true Holy of Holies.
It must have been in heaven where it was invested with

its full supernatural powers.

We have to remember that Jesus was the lamb of sacrifice. He had to shed His blood on our behalf if He was going to redeem us. His blood is the only blood that could have changed our situation. There was no other sacrifice that would have been sufficient. For this sacrifice, we will praise Him forevermore.

We have seen that medical science can keep blood alive for weeks outside the body. The Bible records the fact that Abel's blood spoke from the ground while his body lay lifeless on it. Hebrews records the fact that Jesus' blood spoke after it was released from His body.

So we see that blood can live outside the body, both in medical sense and in a spiritual sense. And it can speak. When the shed blood of righteous men speaks, God listens. Whether the speaking of blood is meant to be taken literally, I will leave to others to debate. I believe it literally, but I would also have no trouble accepting it as an allegory. Either way, I am persuaded that righteous blood communicates with God.

One might argue that they have never heard, or even heard of anyone else hearing of blood speaking. That is probably true, and I would say this: The last thing you would want is for blood to speak to you. You can imagine the effect on those who work in hospitals and mortuaries or slaughterhouses if all of a sudden blood began to speak. But I am persuaded that righteous blood speaks.

In the natural, blood "speaks" to doctors and scientists of various sorts. Just as blood can "tell" doctors a number of things about the health of a patient, or the forensic scientist a number of things about the death of a cadaver, blood says things to God. Blood has life. It can communicate and it has a sensitivity far beyond what we have previously understood.

Gen. 4:10-11:

And he said, what hast thou done? the voice of thy brother's blood crieth unto me from the ground.

And now art thou cursed from the earth, which hath opened her mouth to receive thy brother's blood from thy hand.

Obviously, an all-knowing, all-seeing God was aware of Cain's act of fratricide. This crime was so graphic and so horrific and so foreign to any earthly experience up to that point, that all of creation must have recoiled from it. In one generation man had degenerated so much under the curse of sin that he had gone from Adam's transgression in the Garden to murder by his firstborn son.

Trumbull, in *The Blood Covenant,* tells us that it is not just Abel's memory that is being spoken of here, but it is Abel's self — his soul, his life, his blood that is speaking. In other words, it is the true Abel. Communicating blood, Trumbull points out, was not unknown among primitive people. There have been recorded instances of it down through the ages. He writes: "... in all ages blood unjustly spilled has been supposed to have the power of making its voice heard against him who poured it out by violence." [2]

Trumbull cites one instance in both the Jerusalem and Babylonian Talmuds, which records that the blood of prophet Zechariah, who was slain by King Joash in the temple, would not be quiet but continued to bubble many days after his death.[3] Jesus' own words in Matthew would seem to give some acknowledgment to this idea.

Matt. 23:29-35:

Woe unto you, scribes and Pharisees, hypocrites! because ye build the tombs of the prophets, and garnish the sepulchres of the righteous,

And say, If we had been in the days of our fathers, we would not have been partakers with them in the blood of the prophets.

Wherefore ye be witnesses unto yourselves, that ye are the children of them which killed the prophets.

Fill ye up then the measure of your fathers.

Ye serpents, ye generation of vipers, how can ye escape the damnation of hell?

Wherefore, behold, I send unto you prophets, and wise men, and scribes: and some of them ye shall kill and crucify; and some of them shall ye scourge in your synagogues, and persecute them from city to city:

That upon you may come all the righteous blood shed upon the earth, from the blood of righteous Abel unto the blood of Zacharias son of Barachias, whom ye slew between the temple and the altar.

By mentioning the blood of Zechariah in the same sentence with the blood of Abel, Jesus is telling us that there is a similarity between them. We know that they both had righteous blood, and that both had their blood shed on the earth by unjust men. But I believe that another similarity is that both their blood "spoke" in their death.

Second Recorded Breach In Creation

Abel's murder was the second gaping wound in God's creation. The first was Adam's transgression, but nothing like Abel's death had ever occurred before. It wasn't worse than Adam's transgression. Adam's act had spawned the murder by Cain. It was a direct result. But the earth, up to that point, had never received human blood. It is not inconceivable that Abel's blood was actually shrieking to God in horror and unbelief, saying, "Look, God! Look at what Cain has done! Avenge me!" Abel's murder is the first mention of blood in the Bible, and the Amplified Bible tells us in Hebrews that his blood cried out for vengeance.

I don't believe that innocent blood would cry out for vengeance, but righteous blood would. We know that after the Fall, no human blood was innocent, because of man's consciousness of sin. Animals don't have this consciousness, so their blood would not seek vengeance. Their blood is innocent.

In Hebrews, we have a record of Jesus' blood speaking.

Heb. 12:24:

> **And to Jesus the mediator of the new covenant, and to the blood of sprinkling, that speaketh better things than that of Abel.**

The Amplified Bible is even more explicit:

> **And to Jesus, the Mediator — Go-between, Agent — of a new covenant, and to the sprinkled blood which speaks [of mercy,] a better and nobler and more gracious message than the blood of Abel [which cried out for vengeance].** (AMP)

Again, the skeptic might argue that the word *speaks* here is merely emblematic of what Jesus' blood stood for. It stood for mercy, a mercy so great that He even asked forgiveness for His executioners as He was dying on the cross. Any true believer would have no problem accepting such an allegory of blood speaking.

It could be that the shedding of the blood of other just men has been as horrible to God, but it is reasonable to think that no deaths could have been more painful to the Father than the deaths of Abel and Jesus. Since Abel was a righteous man and the first man to die physically, his death could be viewed as a real setback for the plan of God. But an all-wise, all-knowing God, had foreseen not only Cain's wickedness but the wickedness of those who would cry out for Jesus' blood. Still, Jesus was God's own son manifested in the flesh and the terrible agony of His death must have been quite painful to the Father.

There was one great important difference between Jesus and Abel's death: with Jesus' death came redemption. Abel's death only pushed man deeper into an abyss of sin from which he would always try to extricate himself. Abel became the first man to die, but Jesus became the firstborn from the dead.

Abel Was An Exceptional Man

Clearly, there was something exceptional about Abel. He apparently had a good relationship with his Creator because his sacrifice was found pleasing and acceptable. Abel brought a good sacrifice, and he did so in faith and in devout worship. Cain, his brother, was simply following a routine, and there was no faith or devotion in what he did.

Genesis 4:3 tells us that Cain "brought of the fruit of

the ground an offering unto the Lord." There is nothing special indicated here — just some vegetables grabbed from the pea patch. But Abel, in Genesis 4:4, brought of the "firstlings of his flock and of the fat (or richest part) thereof. And the Lord had respect unto Abel and to his offering."

Undoubtedly, both men knew of the blood sacrifice. If Abel knew, then Cain knew. It is certain that Adam knew, and he would have trained his sons. As young men, growing up, they would have helped him prepare the sacrifice. They would have known that it took blood to cover their sins. But Cain refused to offer blood, and when his offering of vegetation was not accepted, his countenance fell. He let the sin that was lying by the door of his heart overtake him and have rulership over him. Then, rather than repenting and making the changes he needed to make, he turned on Abel and killed him.

1st John 3:12:

> **Not as Cain, who was of that wicked one,
> and slew his brother. And wherefore slew
> he him? Because his own works were evil,
> and his brother's righteous.**

This excerpt from Marilyn Hickey's book, *The Power of the Blood: A Physician's Analysis* (which is not to be confused with H.A. Maxwell Whyte's book by a similar name), is instructive:

> "The second reference [in Genesis] to blood is the sacrifice to God made by Abel, the son of Adam and Eve. Abel, a shepherd, offered God the sacrifice of a lamb. Cain, his brother and a tiller of the soil, offered fruits and vegetables that he had

grown. God accepted Abel's sacrifice, but rejected Cain's.

"In past readings of that account, I have argued, 'God, that was unfair! Cain was a farmer and Abel raised animals. Doesn't it seem only right that the farmer should bring what he had raised?'

"One day while reading Hebrews 11, I realized why God rejected Cain's sacrifice. This passage says that *'by faith'* Abel offered a better sacrifice than Cain. And Romans 10:17 says that *'. . .faith cometh by hearing . . . .'* Abel had heard God's Word and therefore knew that only a blood sacrifice was acceptable to God. If Abel knew that, then so did Cain; but he ignored what he was told by offering the fruit of the ground — the very ground that had been *cursed* by God. Cain's offering displeased God because it was a sacrifice produced from human effort rather than complete faith in God's provision." [4]

We know also that God considered Abel a righteous man because we have Jesus' own words concerning him in Matthew 23:35:

> **That upon you may come all the righteous blood shed upon the earth, from the *blood of righteous Abel* unto the blood of Zacharias son of Barachias, whom ye slew between the temple and the altar.**

Many view Abel, the shepherd, as a type of Christ.

Cain is viewed as a type of the flesh, expecting God to be pleased with his works, his human effort. I find no record of Cain ever atoning for his offenses to God — either the sin of not offering blood, or the sin of shedding his brother's blood. I believe God would have included such an important event in His Word if Cain ever did. Cain apparently never sought repentance.

Satan must have felt sure that he had succeeded in a second preemptive strike against God. First, he got Adam to transgress, and then he instituted the murder of Adam's second son by his first son. What he didn't see or could not know is that God had anticipated these moves, and there would be blood available to cover them.

A lamb had been slain before the foundation of the world.

Law of Purity in Blood:

(Jesus' blood is pure; What is pure exists forever.)

Law of Sanctification in Blood:

(Heavenly acts of sanctification are permanently established in earth and heaven.)

Major points:

1. Jesus' blood didn't die, though His flesh did.

2. Jesus' blood is pure, and what is pure cannot die.

3. We must be sprinkled by faith, not by actual blood.

4. Blood can live outside the body.

5. Blood can communicate.

6. Abel was a type of Christ.

FIVE

BLOOD AND THE HOLY SPIRIT

I believe blood is a type of the Holy Spirit. It appears in the place of spirit. Before Adam sinned he was clothed in a spirit covering of glory. After he sinned, Adam's spiritual covering lifted, and blood — the blood of animals — became his covering.

I believe that the glory had been manifested as Adam's covering by his constant communion with Jesus in the Garden. This came to me as revelation from the Holy Spirit Himself. Now when I read John 6:63, I see it in a whole new light:

> **It is the spirit that quickeneth; the flesh profiteth nothing: the** *words that I speak unto you, they are spirit, and they are life.*

In other words, the words that God speaks to us feeds and enlarges our spirits, just as it did to Adam's spirit. Adam's spirit was so developed that it manifested outwardly as glory. The Lord Himself was speaking with Adam daily, and daily his spirit was being edified or quickened. Adam's spirit was of the same substance as God, and the glory that surrounded Adam was the same as God's glory. It covered his flesh. But when he sinned, life retreated from the spiritually prominent position as his covering to an inferior position in the blood of his physical body. The spirit became changed, lifeless, dormant; but his physical life remained. Animal blood was then shed to provide both a spiritual and a physical covering.

Don't get me wrong. I'm not saying blood is a person like the Holy Spirit, but it does have some of the same characteristics. What other substance has the same ubiquity in our human bodies as the Holy Spirit has in the Body of Christ? The Holy Spirit is in every member of the Body of Christ at the same time. He can flow through and saturate the whole body simultaneously. Likewise, blood flows through and saturates every member of our physical body.

Every Member Bathed In The Spirit

Blood is everywhere in our bodies at once. Prick any member, any portion of skin at any time, and see if blood won't appear. It is not that the Holy Spirit has the liquidity of blood; it is that blood has abilities somewhat like the Holy Spirit. Just as the Holy Spirit can, liquid-like, bathe every member of the Body in spirit-life, so blood can bathe every cell and organ of the body with physical life. Because the life of the flesh is in it (Lev. 17:11).

Blood is the seat of life in our physical bodies; the Holy Spirit is (or will be) the seat of life in our glorified bodies — just as He was in the glory that surrounded Adam.

As long as Adam's spirit was manifested from the inside to the outside, God was able to commune with Adam, Spirit to spirit and Face to face. But when Adam's spirit died and life retreated inside to the blood, God could no longer walk and talk with Adam Spirit to spirit or Face to face, because God cannot commune with mere flesh. It is the spirit that quickens (makes alive), not the flesh (John 6:63), and the Bible tells us that no flesh can glory in His presence (1st Cor. 1:29).

Blood mimics the Holy Spirit. It carries life in its duality, both the spiritual and the physical. Life is the Word — "...the words that I speak unto, they are spirit, and they are life," Jesus said — and the Word is nourishment. The Word is our bread and our oxygen. The Bible tells us that man shall not live by bread (physical food) *alone,* but by every word (spirit food) that proceeds from the mouth of God. The term *alone,* indicates that it is possible for man to subsist, at least for a time, on physical bread, but that is clearly not the only thing God desires man to subsist on. We can live purely carnal (physical) lives, but God wants man to subsist on His Word primarily. When we begin to subsist primarily on His Word, all the physical needs are taken care of. Adam did not have to toil for a living until he lost his spirit covering, for then he was estranged from Word.

John 6:63:

> **It is the spirit that quickeneth; the flesh profiteth nothing: the words that I speak unto you, they are *spirit*, and they are *life*.**

Prov. 4: 20-22:

> **My son, attend to my words; incline thine ear unto my sayings.**

> **Let them not depart from thine eyes; keep them in the midst of thine heart.**

> **For they are life unto those that find them, and health to all their flesh.**

The Holy Spirit comes to bring the revelation of Jesus' words because those words are life. And the words that Jesus spoke are words that came from the Father, because Jesus only said what He heard the Father say. Jesus' words are life. He *is* the Word of life. As we commune with the Word, we commune with life.

Blood is *not* life, but it is the carrier of life. Life is the Spirit and the Word. Remember, it was spirit that God breathed into Adam's nostrils when he became a living soul (Gen. 2:7).

Blood causes our bodies to receive our physical nutrients. Without blood, no part of the body would ever be nourished. Without blood, no part of the body would require nourishment, because the body would have no life.

The Holy Spirit brings our spirits heavenly nourishment. Without the Holy Spirit our human spirits would not be quickened to receive nourishment of the Word.

It may seem that I am talking in circles, but I am trying to drive home a point: What the Spirit does in the

Body of Christ, blood does in our physical bodies. Blood's function is a copy of the Holy Spirit's function. They are about as parallel as two functions can be.

One of the Holy Spirit's roles is protection. When there is a breach, a hole, a wound in the Body of Christ, the Holy Spirit is the only one who can heal that wound. He mends the breach by moving on the hearts of men and causing them to patch up their differences, whether doctrinal or otherwise. It is the Holy Spirit alone who is breaking down the walls of denominational division in the Church and bringing it into accord with the Word of God.

When there is a breach or wound in our physical bodies, blood is the only source of healing. The body would have no capacity to mend itself without blood. Through chemical reactions, blood signals certain defensive forces, prompting them to respond to the need. Blood then develops a protective covering around the wound and allows healing to take place.

The protective covering, or scab, seals the wound. Even the sealing is like the work of the Holy Spirit. To seal means to "stamp for security or preservation, to seal up, or to stop," according to *Strong's Exhaustive Concordance of the Bible.*

Eph. 1:13:

> **In whom [God] ye also trusted after that ye heard the word of truth, the gospel of your salvation: in whom also after that ye believed, ye were sealed with that holy Spirit of promise.**

Eph. 4:30:

> **And grieve not the holy Spirit of God,**

**whereby ye are sealed unto the day of re-
demption.**

Blood never stops moving; as it moves, it patches up
wounds and seals them.

If it ever stops doing either, we would eventually die.
If it leaks out of our bodies, we die.

By the same token, the Holy Spirit never slumbers
nor sleeps. He cannot leak out of us, because we are
sealed, but He can be grieved to the point of not being
able to respond to our needs. When He is taken out of
the earth, we go with Him. Otherwise, turn the lights
out; The ball game is over.

I use Benny Hinn's book, *The Blood*, to piggy-back
my idea on a point that he was making:

> "Later God began to reveal to me through
> His Word that it was the shed blood of
> Christ that made it possible for the Holy
> Spirit to descend.
>
> ". . . Remember that the Lord purchased
> man's redemption by His . . . death and
> resurrection, then ascended to His father
> and there presented the blood which was
> the evidence of redemption.
>
> ". . . When the Father accepted the blood,
> I believe Christ Jesus received from the
> Father the gift of the Holy Spirit to pour
> out upon those who believed in Him." [1]

Benny Hinn's point is not only that the "Holy Spirit
is on earth to enable us to live the Christian life," but
that He manifests Himself where the blood of Jesus is
honored. Of course Benny Hinn is right. But I also be-

lieve that blood represents and *copies* the work of the Holy Spirit.

I believe the Holy Spirit manifests Himself where not only the blood of Jesus is honored, but also where the name of Jesus and the Word, which is Jesus, are honored as well. He is in agreement with all three. Why? Because they all represent Jesus, and they all come together in the blood. So I see blood as a stand-in for the spirit.

A Perfect Picture Of The Holy Spirit's Work

Blood is silent like the Holy Spirit, always moving, always nourishing, never blowing its own horn, but quietly and efficiently going about its life-giving, life-sustaining course unseen.

I believe blood's work in our bodies is an almost perfect picture of the work of the Holy Spirit. In spite of all the knowledge that science has gained about physical blood over the last few hundred years, I am persuaded that if at any point a team of the best blood scientists had sat down with a group of anointed Bible teachers and prayer warriors and decided to work together to understand blood, they would have been shocked by the similarities between blood and the Holy Spirit. Science would have advanced just that much further by such a meeting. The Church would have, too; the spiritual and the physical must work together. But of course, few had the knowledge to do that then. Maybe that is a promise that the future holds.

The thing that neither the Church nor science has ever understood is that blood is more than just a mysterious substance, it is a supernatural substance. It flows between two worlds, both the spirit and the physical.

There is nothing else like it in the universe. The only thing one can compare it to is the Holy Spirit. Blood is truly a treasure in our earthen vessels.

Major points:

1.   Blood is a type of the Holy Spirit.

2.   After Adam sinned, life retreated from his spirit to his blood.

3.   Blood is not life, but it is the carrier of life.

4.   Blood is an imitator of the Holy Spirit.

5.   The Holy Spirit manifests where the Blood of Jesus, the name of Jesus and the Word are honored.

6.   Blood is a supernatural substance.

SIX

THE BLOOD CURSE

The Old World was a pit of sin, so God took the only family He could work with and two of each kind of animal and put them into the ark, and condemned everyone and everything else. After unleashing the Great Flood, he pulled the plug, and everything that wasn't in the ark gurgled down the drain.

With the Old World gone, God told Noah, in Genesis 9:3-6:

The Blood Curse

Every moving thing that liveth shall be meat for you; even as the green herb have I given you all things.

But flesh with the life thereof, which is the blood thereof, shall ye not eat.

And surely your blood of your lives will I require; at the hand of every beast will I require it, and at the hand of man; at the hand of every man's brother will I require the life of man.

Whoso sheddeth man's blood, by man shall his blood be shed: for in the image of God made he man.

The verses emphasize the sanctity of blood. God will seek retribution against any man or any animal that sheds man's blood, for blood represents life. For such an act, He says, ". . . surely your blood of your lives will I require." I believe that God was not only concerned with brother killing brother in vengeance and anger, but in the offering of human sacrifice.

Such sacrifices were evident all over the ancient world. This may have been part of the background that Abraham left when God called him out of Ur of the Chaldees. We know that several biblical cultures offered children to the god Molech. The sacrifices were slowly burned to death in the arms of this idol. Manasseh offered up his son to Molech, and Solomon erected an altar to it.

Human sacrifice was a worldwide concept at that time. As part of the sacrifice came the idea that communion with the gods could be achieved through drinking the blood and eating the flesh of the sacrifice. We know now that what was achieved was communion with demons. For the most part, the sacrifice was an animal, but the highest form of sacrifice was human. Animal sacrifices, while numerous, were considered secondary.

After man fell in the Garden, and his spirit died, God emphasized blood as the covering for sin. Animals, of course, had the only innocent blood because man's blood had been defiled by sin. Man's nature had become sinful, but animals had no concept of sin. These creatures were not aware of sin, so their blood became important to the various offerings of the people and for spiritual cleansing. Animals became man's sacrificial stand-in. Their flesh could be eaten, but not the blood.

Israel Knew Of God's Prohibition

Only Israel knew God's prohibition against eating or drinking blood, while many other cultures were in darkness concerning it. Worshippers in some cultures continue to drink the blood of their sacrifice even today. If Israel had done that, they would have drunk damnation to themselves, because, unlike the heathens of the world, they had the oracles of God.

God said He would require an accounting of man's blood, whether it be shed by beast or by man. This is quite a statement, which men seem to not have heeded then and is almost completely forgotten today. In other words, man never needs to seek vengeance. If God says He will require an accounting of the shedding of man's blood, who is man to exact vengeance? So when Abel's blood cried out for vengeance, it was only crying out for what was legally just. But vengeance certainly would not have aided man.

Men seeking and carrying out vengeance short-circuits God's mercy on the one hand, or His judgment on the other. Yet, when we look at all the murders that are committed daily around the world as acts of revenge, and all the gang retribution, we know that this commandment of not seeking vengeance goes unheeded. Whole nations go to war as acts of revenge. But vengeance belongs to God alone. God says He will recompense man, because man is made in His image. God will allow justice to be played out, but He always gives man a place to repent.

God's focus is on the blood, not the flesh — ("That no flesh should glory in His presence." — 1 Cor. 1: 29.) It is as if God regarded the flesh only as an instrument to transport blood and do works. These verses in Romans 8 throw light on the subject of the flesh:

Rom. 8:3-8

> **For what the law could not do, in that it was weak through the flesh, God sending his own Son in the likeness of sinful flesh, and for sin** [or by a sacrifice of sin], **condemned sin in the flesh:**

> **That the righteousness of the law might be fulfilled in us, who walk not after the flesh, but after the Spirit.**

> **For they that are after the flesh do mind the things of the flesh; but they that are after the Spirit the things of the Spirit.**

> **For to be carnally minded is death; but to be spiritually minded is life and peace.**

> **Because the carnal mind is enmity against God: for it is not subject to the law of God, neither indeed can be.**
>
> **So then they that are in the flesh** [or who cater to carnal desires of the flesh] **cannot please God.**

Blood represents life. Without blood there is only death. The shedding of blood, or the taking of life wantonly or unjustly, opens the door for the curse. Adam's transgression in the Garden allowed a generalized curse to come upon all of God's creation. Cain's transgression in shedding his brother's blood allowed the curse to come upon man himself. Because Cain refused to repent, his blood had to be separated from the blood of other men. God sent him off to the land of Nod, away from Seth through whom God would bring His bloodline.

While God has given man dominion over the earth and over all animal life, He has reserved the blood for Himself. Blood enjoys a sanctity that the flesh does not enjoy.

Lev. 7:26-27:

> **Moreover ye shall eat no manner of blood, whether it be of fowl or of beast, in any of your dwellings.**
>
> **Whatsoever soul it be that eateth any manner of blood, even that soul shall be cut off from his people.**

Lev. 17:14:

> **...Ye shall eat the blood of no manner of**

94

flesh: for the life of all flesh is the blood thereof: whosoever eateth it shall be cut off.

Although under the New Covenant we are released from the laws and restrictions of the Old Covenant which God made with the children of Israel, the prohibition against eating blood still stands. In Acts 15:29, the Jerusalem apostles outlined some "necessary things" from which the Gentile Christians had to refrain themselves.

That ye abstain from meats offered to idols, and from [eating] blood, and from things strangled, and from fornication.

What we are seeing indicated by these verses is that there is a difference between the flesh and the blood. Life itself is carried by the blood. Ultimately, the blood of Jesus became the sanctifier of every man who would accept God's redemption, just as animal blood was used to sanctify Israel before Jesus came.

Ex. 24:6-8:

And Moses took half of the blood, and put it in basons; and half of the blood he sprinkled on the altar.

And he took the book of the covenant, and read in the audience of the people: and they said, All that the Lord hath said will we do, and be obedient.

And Moses took the blood, and sprinkled it on the people, and said, Behold the blood of the covenant, which the Lord hath made with you concerning all these words.

Half the blood was sprinkled on the altar and the other half was sprinkled on the people. This was a way that God had chosen of sanctifying his people, and a way of demonstrating unity with them.

(I always have trouble trying to imagine Moses sprinkling blood on church people today. How many of us would put up with having blood slung on our designer suits and dresses? Of course, those were different times, but Moses did that to the people and sanctified them. Maybe today we would rather be clean and fashionable than sanctified. Thank God, that because of Jesus' shed blood on behalf of every man, there is no need for another animal sacrifice. Thank God that all the sprinkling today is by faith.)

In Exodus 12 is a very familiar passage of Scripture. God tells Israel He will "pass through the land of Egypt this night, and will smite all the firstborn in the land of Egypt" as a judgment against that nation. God had been very patient with Egypt, though they had shed the blood of His chosen people for hundreds of years. Now it was time for deliverance and judgment. Pharaoh, a vengeful and prideful tyrant, refused to let the children of Israel leave to worship their God in the wilderness.

So God smote the waters of Egypt, which is the life of the land, and turned them to blood. This included the Nile River, considered sacred by Egyptians.

Ex. 7:21:

And the fish that was in the river died; and the river stank, and the Egyptians could not drink of the water of the river; and there was blood throughout all the land of Egypt.

The bloody rivers and streams should have been

enough of a signal to Pharaoh that he could not win in a head-on clash with the God of Israel, but this obstinate king was a picture of the kind of God-resisting, prejudiced nation that Egypt was. They were a powerful nation determined to do just as they pleased, including oppress the people of God.

This foul-smelling plague of blood stood for the curse of death that was upon the nation. I believe this blood represented judgment for the generations of innocent (not sinless) people whose blood had been shed by Egypt's Pharaohs. We can see here the Law of Sin and Blood in full expression. The law says, Where there is sin, there must be blood. In Egypt, blood flowed like a mighty river. It brings to mind the words of Jesus:

Matt. 23:35:

That upon you may come all the righteous blood shed upon the earth ...

Pharaoh refused to release God's people. The obstinate king put his nation through eight other devastating plagues — the plague of frogs, the plague of lice, the plague of flies, the plague of cattle, the plague of boils, the plague of hail, the plague of locusts, and the plague of darkness — simply because he was too proud to repent.

Finally, God instructed the children of Israel to take the blood of the lamb and strike it on the two side posts and on the upper door posts of their houses. He was about to allow the last plague — the death of all Egypt's firstborn. In Exodus 12: 13, it says:

And the blood shall be to you for a token upon the houses where ye are: and when I see the blood, I will pass over you, and the

plague shall not be upon you to destroy you, when I smite the land of Egypt.

Verse 22:

And ye shall take a bunch of hyssop, and dip it in the blood that is in the bason, and strike the lintel and the two side posts with the blood that is in the bason: and none of you shall go out at the door of his house until the morning.

We know the miraculous result. The lambs' blood protected the children of Israel, but all the firstborn of Egypt were killed, even Pharaoh's own son. Just as the lambs' blood protected the children of Israel, so the blood of the Lamb protects the children of God today. As we can see in Exodus 24:6-8, the blood of animals was used to seal God's covenant with the children of Israel, but the Christian's covenant is sealed in the blood of Jesus, the Lamb of God.

1st Peter 1:18-20:

Forasmuch as ye know that ye were not redeemed with corruptible things, as silver and gold, from your vain conversation received by tradition from your fathers;

But with the precious blood of Christ, as of a lamb without blemish and without spot:

Who verily was foreordained before the foundation of the world, but was manifest in these last times for you.

The blood that we were redeemed with is not something that is corruptible, as are silver and gold. It will not die or stink or change. It is pure, incorruptible. And yet we see how the world spends itself daily trying to obtain gold and silver, when all the time the blood of Jesus is much more precious, and it can be theirs just for the asking.

God Sometimes Requires Blood

God may require the shedding of blood for spiritual reasons, as in the case of his covenant partner Abraham. One day God told Abraham to make a sacrifice of Isaac to prove his commitment. If Abraham had withheld his only son, would not God have been justified in withholding His only son? But Abraham was a man of faith. He believed that if God required Isaac's life, He would restore that life to him.

God may require blood, as in the case of Achan at Jericho. When Achan chose the accursed things, he became a curse. Achan became the same type of person that God had sent Israel to destroy. He was no longer fit to be of godly service, or to live among God's people. Achan, like the people of Jericho, had to be destroyed.

Again, in Gen. 4: 10-11, we see that Cain becomes cursed when he shed Abel's blood. Even the ground that Cain had tilled would no longer yield its strength to him, because Cain had shed his brother's blood on it.

> **And he** (God) **said, What hast thou done? the voice of thy brother's blood crieth unto me from the ground.**

> **And now art thou cursed from the earth, which hath opened her mouth to receive thy brother's blood from thy hand;**

There were specific times when God required the shedding of blood:

> He required blood as an atonement for sin.

> He required blood in vengeance for the shedding of blood.

> He required blood for sanctification.

When God required blood for spiritual cleansing, it was always the blood of bulls, goats, rams, birds and various other animals. To redeem man once and for all, the blood of an innocent man was required. But there was no such blood existing in the earth, and it had not existed since Adam. It took the act of an innocent man to put man in his sinful predicament, and it would take the act of an innocent man to bring man out of it. Nothing else could satisfy the demands of divine justice. The blood of bulls and goats would no longer suffice, and all human blood at that time was tainted by sin. So God had to provide for Himself a Lamb of sacrifice. Jesus became the Lamb of God which taketh away the sin of the world.

Major Points:

1. Israel had the oracles of God concerning the drinking of blood, but the rest of the world did not.

2. God has reserved the blood for Himself.

3. Man is forbidden to seek blood in revenge.

4. Divine justice may sometimes require the shedding of man's blood.

SEVEN

THE COMMUNION
IN BLOOD

Take, eat: this is my body, which is broken for you: this do in remembrance of me.

. . . This cup is the new testament in my blood: this do ye, as oft as ye drink it, in remembrance of me.

1st Cor. 11:24-25

HOW THE BLOOD WORKS

We celebrate our blood covenant with God in the communion service, but it is clear that though many Christians participate in communion in some form or other, few have more than a superficial grasp of what they are doing and why they are doing it. Because of this lack of knowledge, and lack of historical perspective, they may be doing more harm to themselves than good.

The blood covenant rites, writes H. Clay Trumbull in his book, *The Blood Covenant*, were a "form of mutual covenanting, by which two persons enter into the closest, the most enduring, and the most sacred of compacts, as friends and brothers, or as more than brothers, through the inter-commingling of their blood, by means of its mutual tasting, or of its intertransfusion." [1]

"In marriage," writes Trumbull, "divorce is a possibility: not so in the covenant of blood."[2] ". . . He who has entered into this compact with another, counts himself the possessor of a double life; for his friend, whose blood he has shared, is ready to lay down his life with him, or for him."[3]

In parts of the East, Trumbull explains, the blood covenant is "even a closer tie than that of natural descent." ". . . We, in the West, are accustomed to saying that 'blood is thicker than water'; but the Arabs have the idea that blood is thicker than milk, than a mother's milk. . . .[4] "Arabs hold that brothers in the covenant of blood are closer than brothers at a common breast; that those who have tasted each other's blood are in a surer covenant than those who have tasted the same milk together."[5]

This same type of thinking is confirmed in Paul's letters to the saints at Rome, in which he explains that Israel is not those who can trace their genealogy back to Abraham. These are merely the children of the flesh, and not the children of God, said Paul. The children of God are the children of the promise.

Rom. 9:6-8:

For they are not all Israel, which are of Israel:

Neither, because they are the seed of Abraham, are they all children: but, In Isaac shall thy seed be called.

That is, They which are the children of the flesh, these are not the children of God: but the children of the promise are counted for the seed.

In short, those with whom we share the closest ties are those who have shared in the covenant blood of Jesus with us. In fact, they are not only close to us — they are us, for we are all joined in the same body. To tear apart from one another would be the same as tearing flesh from the human body. Such ties cannot be broken once they are established. In God's economy, the blood of Jesus is indeed "thicker" than either water or mother's milk, for the blood breaks down all divisions between us, joins us in His Body and seals us forever. Those who are joined together in Christ have a kinship with God that goes beyond any possible earthly relationship.

Trumbull shows conclusively that blood covenants in one form or another have been practiced since time immemorial by many cultures. Such covenants are still practiced today in certain primitive societies. These covenants were intended to bind the parties together for generations, usually in a pact of mutual love, friendship, and protection.

The rite, of course, took many, many forms. It most often involved the self-inflicted wounding or cutting of one or each of the parties and allowing the blood to drip into a cup of wine, or water, or some other drink.

(These liquids had their own symbolic meanings. Wine was an invigorating spiritual beverage, that itself symbolized blood. Water was and is a liquid that is necessary for life, and is known for its uses in cleansing and purifying.)

The parties then recited their declarations of faithfulness or mutual aid before drinking the contents. By performing or "cutting" the covenant, the parties were now bound to one another forever; even their families were bound.

Opening Up The Heart Of Africa

It is believed that only by cutting such covenants with tribal chieftains were white men able to open up the heart of Africa to exploration. David Livingstone, the great missionary-explorer-physician of the late 1800s, reportedly cut a number of such covenants with various chiefs. Henry M. Stanley, the American journalist credited with "finding" Livingstone, reportedly cut more than fifty such covenants both during his search for Livingstone and after Livingstone's death.

Although there had been white African explorers before, none had penetrated so deeply into the continent as did Livingstone and, eventually, Stanley. Livingstone's desire was to establish missions in Africa's "dark interior" and to find routes to the coast that would make the slave trade unnecessary.

The rites of blood covenanting, as practiced by these and other primitive societies the world over, are far more sophisticated than the simple rites we Americans have retained.

Intermingled Blood With A Friend

As children we might have intermingled our blood with that of a friend, or even tasted their blood, while we professed friendship forever. Scenes from old western movies might be remembered where two Indians (or an Indian and a paleface) cut their palms with a knife and clasp their hands together while vowing their friend's enemy would be their enemy. While movie images were meant to show indications of strong friendship, those depictions pale beside the strength of the covenants in many Eastern societies.

The covenant that Jesus cut with us is eternally unbreakable, not because we would not break it but because He would not break it. It was an absolutely lopsided deal in that we brought nothing to the altar. Jesus brought Himself and all that is in the Kingdom of God. In other words, He brought all that belonged to Him by inheritance. As is often the case in blood covenants, everything each maker owns comes under the ownership of the other maker. So you can see who benefitted most in our relationship with Christ. Our covenant tells us that everything Jesus has is ours, whether things in heaven or in earth. Jesus offered up Himself on the altar to be sacrificed, and shed His blood for many. Our part is only to accept the sacrifice he made, and be partakers of that blood.

According to Trumbull, men everywhere have longed for God, and the sacrifices to Him have been man's attempt to achieve "inter-union" and "inter-communion" with Him. So that whether "they give of their own blood, or of substitute blood, or they receive its touch," it is "evidence of their desire for oneness of nature with God. They crave communion with God, and they eat of their sacrifices accordingly."[6] He points to Jesus' words in John 6:53-58:

> **Then Jesus said unto them, Verily, verily, I say unto you, Except ye eat the flesh of the Son of man, and drink his blood, ye have no life in you.**
>
> **Whoso eateth my flesh, and drinketh my blood, hath eternal life; and I will raise him up at the last day.**
>
> **For my flesh is meat indeed, and my blood is drink indeed.**
>
> **He that eateth my flesh, and drinketh my blood, dwelleth in me, and I in him.**
>
> **As the living Father hath sent me, and I live by the Father: so he that eateth me, even he shall live by me.**
>
> **This is that bread which came down from heaven: not as your fathers did eat manna, and are dead: he that eateth of this bread shall live for ever.**

It was universally accepted in primitive societies that the sacrifice offered to a god took on the divine nature of that god, and that by eating the sacrifice man took on or assimilated that same nature, writes Trumbull in *The Blood Covenant*. "The blood gave common life; the flesh gave common nourishment."[7]

Jesus, in offering us His flesh and His blood, is offering no less than complete identity with Himself — a common life and a common nourishment, whereby we take on His divine nature. Indeed, if we do not partake of His flesh and blood we have no life in us at all, he said.

The communion man has always craved is oneness with God. Man has always wanted to know his Creator and be joined with Him in complete fellowship and partnership. That is part of the nature of man. This is why men in heathen cultures slay and sacrifice animals and eat their flesh and drink their blood. It is by doing so that they believe they obtain communion with their gods. It is in this manner that they set a table before their gods and invoke their gods' presence.

One can easily see that heathen cultures did not have the true light. Men can only act on what they know, and in ancient days no nation but Israel had the knowledge of the one true God. That is why God did not spare Israel when they sinned in the wilderness by making idol gods and sacrificing to them, for they had been warned.

Ex. 20:2-5:

> **I am the Lord thy God, which have brought thee out of the land of Egypt, out of the house of bondage.**
>
> **Thou shalt have no other gods before me.**
>
> **Thou shalt not make unto thee any graven image, or any likeness of any thing that is in heaven above, or that is in the earth beneath, or that is in the water under the earth:**

Thou shalt not bow down thyself to them, nor serve them: for I the Lord thy God am a jealous God ....

The Scriptures warn us today as well. In 1st Corinthians 10:7, we read:

Neither be ye idolaters, as were some of them; as it is written, The people sat down to eat and drink, and rose up to play.

In other words, the people offered sacrifices to false gods, ate and drank of the sacrifices, and proceeded immediately into orgiastic lusting and carnality. When the light of the Gospel is missing from worship even today, perversion of some type is often the result. Verses 8-10 continue:

Neither let us commit fornication, as some of them committed, and fell in one day three and twenty thousand.

Neither let us tempt Christ, as some of them also tempted, and were destroyed of serpents.

Neither murmur ye, as some of them also murmured, and were destroyed of the destroyer.

What we're seeing in these passages is the destruction that Israel brought upon themselves after having been joined first to God Almighty, and then joining themselves to idol gods. They were literally joined — married, if you will — to Almighty God, but they began lusting for other gods. The word *fornication* thus takes on a double meaning as that of practicing idolatry as well as

108

having unlawful sex.

1st Cor. 10:14-18:

> **Wherefore, my dearly beloved, flee from idolatry.**
>
> **I speak as to wise men; judge ye what I say.**
>
> **The cup of blessing which we bless, is it not the communion of the blood of Christ? The bread which we break, is it not the communion of the body of Christ?**
>
> **For we being many are one bread, and one body: for we are all partakers of that one bread.**
>
> **Behold Israel after the flesh: are not they which eat of the sacrifices partakers of the altar?**

Here God is asking the question, one that we must seriously consider every time we take communion: Aren't we partakers of His blood and His body when we drink of the cup and eat of the bread? The answer, of course, is yes, we are joined with Him spiritually. We have become one bread and one body. Now He asks, "Behold Israel after the flesh: are not they which eat of the sacrifices partakers of the altar?" The answer again is yes. When Israel ate from the sacrifice offered to idols, they became a partaker of that table, which was not the Lord's table. Israel joined themselves with other gods, so the one true God had to remove His covering of protection.

Verses 19-20:

> **What say I then? that the idol is any thing,**

or that which is offered in sacrifice to idols is any thing?

But I say, that the things which the Gentiles sacrifice, they sacrifice to devils, and not to God: and I would not that ye should have fellowship with devils.

No, the idol is nothing in actuality but wood or stone (or money, sex , or fame) or whatever material or obsession man uses to fashion his idol. These things can neither walk, nor talk, nor run, nor laugh, nor hear, nor aid anyone. They are dependent on man to carve, sculpt, build or animate them. If man doesn't carry them, they cannot get from one place to another. These idols are dependent on man for the very form they take. It would be the same if you were a potter and sat down and made a large, elaborate pot, painted it gaily, put on a glaze, fired it in a kiln until the glaze became hard, and then decided to worship it. The act of worship doesn't make the pot a god. It is still a pot. But the act of worshipping makes you an idolater.

God Almighty can walk, talk, hear, and create people and then sustain His creation. No one made Him, but He made all things. He is pre-existent of all things. He is self-sustaining, and He sustains all other life. He can be in all places at all times. He can take on any form that He likes. He exists whether we worship Him or not, so it is foolish not to worship Him. It is even more foolish for man to bow down to an idol, which can do nothing of itself. Even that which is sacrificed to idols is nothing but an animal of some type that God gave to befriend or entertain us, or to provide us with food and clothing, or to do work on our behalf.

Sacrifice Is Worth More Than The Idol

The epitome of folly in the case of idols is that the animal, or the sacrifice, is often worth more than the god for whom it is sacrificed. At least the animal is alive. It can move, do work for us and be of use as a pet, as food and as clothing, while the idol can do nothing. But are we to worship animals? Of course not! Yet some people do.

It is the act of sacrificing to someone or something other than God that determines ones fidelity. Clearly, Israel's fidelity was lacking. Israel was putting other gods before God himself, and that is a no-no.

What follows now is the clincher:

Verse 21:

Ye cannot drink the cup of the Lord, and the cup of devils: ye cannot be partakers of the Lord's table, and of the table of devils.

We cannot have communion with the Lord and communion with devils at the same time. A decision has to be made; we cannot have it both ways. When we try to have both we might as well get ready for problems, because it tears apart the Body and we have cut ourselves off from God's protection. The true God must always remove Himself from such a situation. When we worship or sacrifice to another god, we have eaten and drunken damnation to ourselves. It is not God that brings the damnation, but we do.

I see all the time how some people try to partake of the Lord's table and the table of devils. They want to dabble in mysticism, psychic phenomena, and New Age

111

cults, and then have the audacity to take communion at church. Throughout the Caribbean and parts of South America, we see how people try to blend Jesus together with voodoo and other demonic practices. It just doesn't work, and in some cases the people may not know any better. They do it in ignorance.

Today, thank God, we do not have to bring animal sacrifices. Once the sacrifice was established in heaven, it was established for all time. There will never be a need for another sacrifice — or any other sacrificial blood. All we have to do now is remember periodically that the sacrifice has been made and that Jesus became the Lamb of sacrifice. Paul says in 1st Corinthians 11: 23-34:

> **For I have received of the Lord that which also I delivered unto you, That the Lord Jesus the same night in which he was betrayed took bread:**

> **And when he had given thanks, he brake it, and said, Take, eat: this is my body, which is broken for you: this do in remembrance of me.**

> **After the same manner also he took the cup, when he had supped, saying, This cup is the new testament in my blood: this do ye, as oft as ye drink it, in remembrance of me.**

> **For as often as ye eat this bread, and drink this cup, ye do show the Lord's death till he come.**

> **Wherefore whosoever shall eat this bread, and drink this cup of the Lord, unworthily**

[not in reverence], **shall be guilty of the body and blood of the Lord.**

But let a man examine himself, and so let him eat of that bread, and drink of that cup.

For he that eateth and drinketh unworthily, eateth and drinketh damnation to himself, not discerning the Lord's body.

For this cause many are weak and sickly among you, and many sleep.

For if we would judge ourselves, we should not be judged.

But when we are judged, we are chastened of the Lord, that we should not be condemned with the world.

Wherefore, my brethren, when ye come together to eat, tarry one for another.

And if any man hunger, let him eat at home; that ye come not together unto condemnation. And the rest will I set in order when I come.

Major points:

1. Few Christians understand communion.

2. Whoever shares familial blood is a relative. Whoever shares covenant blood is closer than a relative; He is a brother in Christ.

3. Blood covenants can never be broken.

113

4.   Sacrifices have been man's attempt to achieve communion with their gods.

5.   By eating the sacrifice, man takes on the nature of his god.

6.   We cannot have communion with God and devils.

EIGHT

PLEADING THE BLOOD

Blood will concentrate in the body where it is most needed. When conditions in the body demand the application of more blood, the blood dutifully responds. If there is an attack on any area of the physical body, blood rushes to the area to start the healing — be it a wound, an infection or a bruise — and to cleanse the area. Blood always responds to the body's call. Likewise, we in the Body of Christ must call for the application of the blood of Christ where and when it is needed.

Let me give you an example.

1 John 1:7-9:

> **But if we walk in the light, as he is in the light, we have fellowship one with another, and the blood of Jesus Christ his Son cleanseth us from all sin.**
>
> **If we say that we have no sin, we deceive ourselves, and the truth is not in us.**
>
> **If we confess our sins, he is faithful and just to forgive us our sins, and to cleanse us from all unrighteousness.**

When we are walking in the light with the Lord, that Blood is working on our behalf and constantly cleansing us from all sin that we may unwittingly get into. This is rather routine work for the Blood. There could be a thousand things we do or say or think in a day's time that we never give a second thought. Yet, those actions may either be sins or open doors for the enemy. For example, did you know that fear is sin? Lots of Christians are walking masses of fears and phobias. They love the Lord, but they become paralyzed at the sight of cats, or at the thought of flying. They love the Lord, but their conversation is heavily sprinkled with such terms as *I'm afraid* — "I'm afraid I can't go today" or "I'm afraid it's too late" or "I'm afraid I'm going to have to miss this party." They are constantly speaking fear into their lives. So the Blood must constantly work to close these breaches that are opened on a daily basis. These things are under the Blood, we say.

That is exactly what natural blood does in our bodies. It is quietly working, patrolling the blood vessels and tissues, looking for tears in the vessel walls or signs of infection. All day, blood is repairing those openings that we know nothing about. We never see them, never feel them, and are never aware of them. These are tiny ruptures that even a doctor could not detect with his instruments, and yet they are occurring all the time. These tears and infections have nothing to do with overt illness, just as little fears and phobias have nothing to do with overt or conscious thought. They are just there.

The Sin Offering In Israel

(The equivalent of this is the "sin offering" as practiced by biblical Israel. The sin offering, or *chattah*, was an important ritual for the expiation of sins that were committed unwittingly. In the *chattah*, the priest (representing the guilty) laid his hands upon the head of the sacrificial animal, making it their representative, and then he killed it. After it was killed, its blood was sprinkled around the altar and the sacred area to purify the guilty.)

If we say that we have no sin, we deceive ourselves, and the truth is not in us.

We can never say we have no sin, because we sin all the time. We are far less than perfect in dealing with sin than we sometimes think we are.

Besides the unconscious or unwitting sins, we commit little conscious sins all the time. A tiff with our spouse may go unresolved for days; we fail to correct a false impression that someone may have gotten of us because it benefitted us; we watch a television program, knowing that it grieves our spirits but it titillates our flesh. Unlike the unconscious sins, these are sins we are aware of. They

117

happen all the time, and no one is immune to them.

We are not talking murder here, or fornication, or lying on our taxes, or cheating on our spouses, or stealing on the job. We're talking little unconfessed things that no one else knows about, or even if they knew they wouldn't think much of them. And they wouldn't necessarily think less of us if they knew we had committed these acts. They chalk these things up to being human, and they are right. Yet we know in ourselves that they are sins, because the Holy Spirit has dealt with us over and over to straighten them out. Why? Because He is constantly trying to take us higher. He wants to take us to another level with Him, and He can't do that if we are trying to drag along these "little things." It's hard to travel light with the Holy Spirit when we carry so many of these little carnal bags.

If we confess our sins, he is faithful and just to forgive us our sins, and to cleanse us from all unrighteousness.

If we are willing to admit our sins to God and ask His forgiveness, God will forgive us and cleanse us from the unrighteous act. How does He cleanse us? He cleanses us with the blood of Jesus. (I would not argue with someone who says, no, it is the washing of the water of the Word that cleanses us. Ultimately, I make very little distinction between the function of the Blood and the function of the Word, as you shall see.)

What we have just dealt with are two examples of where sins cause openings for the enemy to get in: one is unconscious and the other is conscious. In the unconscious example, the cleansing by the Blood is automatic. In the conscious example, we recognize our faults and ask forgiveness and are then cleansed by the Blood.

There is another provision for a spiritual opening or breach that we should consider. To explain, let's go back to Exodus 12.

Verse 3:

> **Speak ye** [Moses and Aaron] **unto all the congregation of Israel, saying, In the tenth day of this month they shall take to them every man a lamb, according to the house of their fathers, a lamb for an house:**

Verses 21-23:

> **Then Moses called for all the elders of Israel, and said unto them, Draw out and take you a lamb according to your families, and kill the passover.**

> **And ye shall take a bunch of hyssop, and dip it in the blood that is in the bason, and strike the lintel and the two side posts with the blood that is in the bason: and none of you shall go out at the door of his house until the morning.**

> **For the Lord will pass through to smite the Egyptians; and when he seeth the blood upon the lintel, and on the two side posts, the Lord will pass over the door, and will not suffer the destroyer to come in unto your houses to smite you.**

Had the Lord not warned the people of what was going to happen, they could not have known. They could not see into the spirit world. These were not spiritually mature people, so they would not have perceived either the destroyer or God moving among them. If they knew of the destroyer at all, they were much less aware than we are today of how to combat him. They depended on God solely for their information, which came down to them through the prophets.

As Joyce Meyer puts it in her book, *The Word, the Name and the Blood,* there are doors in the spirit world that we know nothing about. If you don't know that a door is open, you won't know to close it. But you can keep all the doors and windows closed, if you apply the Blood daily to the doors and lintels or your life and home. That way, the death angel cannot come in to kill, steal and destroy.

I believe the blood of Jesus actually searches out sin in our lives because the blood in our bodies actually searches out germs and infection. Our blood, especially some of the white blood cells, are very aggressive in their search for disease, toxins and damaged tissue. This action of the blood belies its image of a passive fluid that meekly flows through the body. Conversely, Satan has stepped up his all-out war against blood. Is there any wonder that most of the more devastating diseases on the scene today — AIDS, ebola, cancer and others — are viral diseases that disable the immune cells in the blood?

How much more aggressive than our blood is the blood of Jesus? A million times, a billion times? In the presence of disease and infection, our blood cells multiply very quickly to battle the condition. What this tells us is that Jesus' blood will multiply to the level of need. The greater the need, the greater the blood. Satan and demons are totally overcome by the blood of Jesus, just as infectious germs are overcome by the leukocytes, the germ-fighting element in the white blood cells.

It's The Same Thing With The Word

One might ask, can't I accomplish the same thing by confessing the Word? Sure. I believe the Blood accomplishes the same thing as the Word, but I believe also that the Word and the Blood work together. What you don't get with one you get with another. In using the Word, I believe you have to be much more conscious of directly applying your confessions to every individual area of concern, while you can apply the Blood in areas that you are not always conscious of. By that I mean, if you're standing against sickness, you go to Scriptures that deal with healing. If you're standing against lack, you go to Scriptures that deal with abundance. Whatever you confess the Word over, the enemy cannot get to, as long as you do it by faith. What you fail to cover he can get to. What you don't know about, he can get to.

As I have mentioned, we are not always aware of doors that are open in the spirit world. With the Blood, you can apply it to every area in one brief faith-filled statement:

"Father, I plead (apply) the Blood over my family, my home, my body, my finances, my car, my job. I thank you that they are covered with the Blood right now, in Jesus' name."

In an overall way, that deals with everything at once and locks Satan out. But in dealing with the Blood alone, your mind will not be renewed, nor will you be expressing the creative power that is found uniquely in the Word.

I believe it is good to use the Blood in conjunction with the Word. By this, you're always reminding the Father of His Word in that certain area. Your mind is constantly being renewed by speaking the Word, your spirit-man hears the Word and is fed, and faith comes by hearing that Word. By using the Word in conjunction with the Blood, you're applying faith and creative power while at the same time warding off a lot of unforeseen attacks that the enemy might make. Then, of course, you sign off with the Name of Jesus. The Word, the Name and the Blood. They work together — by faith.

Eccles. 4:12:

And if one prevail against him, two shall withstand him; and a threefold cord is not quickly broken.

The Name we understand; the Word we have begun to understand; the Blood is the third part of that cord that has been missing.

Pleading The Blood Vs. Begging

Many people, when they think of the word *plead* see someone down on their knees with their hands clasped in front of them and sweat pouring down their faces, imploring the Almighty to "please, please, please" do something to help them. That's not pleading; that's begging. And you're right if you think that kind of posture would not be pleasing to God. God does not respond to that kind of activity. God is a faith God, and He responds to faith.

The Bible uses at least four Hebrew words for the word *plead*, and two meanings that seem to pop up consistently are the words *contend* and *strive*. Never do they mean to beg.

But who are we contending and striving with? Certainly not with the Blood, and certainly not with God. We're contending and striving with our enemy, the accuser of the brethren. We use the word *plead* in a legal sense, as we would use it to plead our case in a court of law. In court, we are contending with and striving with the one who would accuse us. We are fighting to stay out of jail, or any other kind of bondage, whether spiritual, mental or physical.

The Blood comes to our defense. The Word comes to our defense. The Name comes to our defense. They all represent Jesus. No enemy, no accuser can stand against either one, let alone all three.

Rev. 12:10-11:

> **And I heard a loud voice saying in heaven, Now is come salvation, and strength, and the kingdom of our God, and the power of his Christ: for the accuser of our brethren is cast down, which accused them before our God day and night.**
>
> **And they overcame him by the blood of the Lamb, and by the word of their testimony; and they loved not their lives unto the death.**

Major points:

1. The Blood cleanses away both unconscious and conscious sins.

2. The Blood closes openings in the spirit world that we are unaware of.

3. The Blood and the Word accomplish the same thing.

4. To plead means to strive and to contend. It does not mean to beg.

NOTES

Chapter 1

1 Maxwell Whyte, *The Power of the Blood* (Springdale, Pa.: Whitaker House, 1973), p. 24.

2 H. Clay Trumbull, *The Blood Covenant* (Kirkwood, Mo.: Impact Christian Books, 1975), All rights reserved. p. 232.

3 Ibid., p. 172.

4 Maxwell Whyte, *The Power of the Blood*, p. 14.

Chapter 2

1 Maxwell Whyte, *The Power of the Blood*, p. 53.

Chapter 4

1 William D. Edwards, MD; Wesley J. Gabel, MDiv; Floyd E. Hosmer, MS, AMI, *On the Physical Death of Jesus Christ*, (Rochester, Minn.: The Mayo Foundation, 1986).

2 Trumbull, *The Blood Covenant*, p. 359.

3 Ibid., p. 360-361.

4 Marilyn Hickey, *The Power of the Blood: A Physician's Analysis*, (Denver, Colo.: Marilyn Hickey Ministries, 1987) p. 20.

Chapter 5

1   Benny Hinn, *The Blood: Its Power From Genesis to Jesus to You*, (Lake Mary, Fla.: Creation House, 1993) pp. 82-83.

Chapter 7

1   Trumbull, *The Blood Covenant*, p. 4.

2   Ibid., p. 6.

3   Ibid., p. 7.

4   Ibid., p. 10.

5   Ibid., p. 11.

6   Ibid., p. 277

7   Ibid., p. 182.

ORDER FORM

Please send _____ copy(ies) of *How The Blood
Works* by Stanley O. Williford to the following
address:

Name:_____

Address:_____

_____

City:_____State:____Zip:_____

Hard cover $14.95
Shipping, per book   2.00
Three-day delivery   4.00

Sales tax, 8.25% (CA)   _____

Total Enclosed   _____

Please make out your check or money order
to Vision Publishing, and mail to:

Vision Publishing
P.O. Box 11166
Carson, Calif. 90746-1166

Please allow three to four weeks for delivery
of your book, unless three-day delivery is
requested.